HOW TO FIND
WORK
in the 21st Century

HOW TO FIND
WORK
in the 21st Century

Ron McGowan

Self-Counsel Press
(a division of)
International Self-Counsel Press Ltd.
Canada   USA

Self-Counsel Press acknowledges the financial support of the Government of Canada through the Book Publishing Industry Development Program (BPIDP) for our publishing activities.

Printed in Canada.

Fifth edition: 2009

Library and Archives Canada Cataloguing in Publication

McGowan, Ron, 1943-
    How to find work in the 21st century / Ron McGowan.

ISBN 978-1-55180-858-1

    1. Job hunting—Handbooks, manuals, etc. I. Title.
HF5382.7.M37 2008   650.14   C2008-906570-0

Self-Counsel Press is committed to protecting the environment and to the responsible use of natural resources. We are acting on this commitment by working with suppliers and printers to phase out our use of paper produced from ancient forests. This book is one step toward that goal. It is printed on 100 percent ancient-forest-free paper (100 percent post-consumer recycled), processed chlorine- and acid-free.

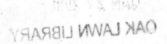

Self-Counsel Press
(a division of)
International Self-Counsel Press Ltd.

1481 Charlotte Road   1704 North State Street
North Vancouver, BC V7J 1H1   Bellingham, WA 98225
Canada   USA

ACKNOWLEDGMENTS

Many thanks to my family and friends for all of their help and support through some challenging times. Without their help, this book would never have been written.

Thanks to all the people I've worked with in Canada, the UK, and Ireland over the past ten years who have taught me so much about the workplace.

Thanks to Karen Aplin-Payton of Aplin Ink Corporate Communications, Naomi Pauls of Paper Trail Publishing, and Peter Bowra of Archer Consulting for their help and professional skills in creating the earlier editions of the book.

NOTICE TO READERS

CONTENTS

Preface   xix

Introduction   xxv

1 How the Workplace Has Changed   1

Looking for Work Instead of a Job   1

  Is that all there is?   1

  The rise of the temporary or contingent worker   2

  Outsourcing   3

  A new relationship   5

  The shift to smaller companies   5

  A new set of expectations   6

  No more entitlements   7

  A need to take the broader view   8

  Facing reality   8

  It's not all bad   9

Most Employment Opportunities Are Hidden   10

  Where are the opportunities?   10

  Finding employment opportunities   11

Why Contracting Makes Sense 13
    Myths about contracting 13
    What employers are looking for 15
Make It Easy to Get Hired 16
    Guess who gets offered the job? 17
    Employee referral programs 17
    Trying before buying 18
The Need for Self-Promotion 19
    Why you have to self-promote 19
    Managing your own career 20
Summary 21
A Note About the Quizzes 22

2 What Exactly Do You Have to Offer? 25
What Is Important and Relevant for You? 25
    Get some help 26
    Be patient with yourself 27
    An ongoing process 28
How Career Fit Are You? 28
Defining Your Personal and Career Profile 29
    Who are you? 29
    What are your values? 31
    Education and training 33
    Weaknesses 34
    Appraising your career 34
    Skills 36
    Achievements 37
    Interests 37
    Types of work 38
    Your career/life highlights and lowlights 39
    Personal life 39

School/college/university 40

Career 41

Summarizing your career 41

Succeeding as a Contractor 43

Market yourself continually 44

Broaden your vision 45

Hone your communication skills 46

Commit to continuous learning 47

Stay on top of the market 47

Go where the action is 48

Watch your finances 49

Avoid stock options 50

Manage your time effectively 50

Increase your physical/mental fitness 51

Practical benefits of exercise 52

Stay flexible 53

3 How to Market Yourself 57

Sales and Marketing Defined 57

Myths About Selling 57

What makes you different? 59

Preparing for an interview or meeting 59

The marketing metaphor 61

Marketing Tools 61

Advertising 61

Design an advertising plan 62

Who are your potential customers? 62

What value are you offering? 63

How much will you charge? 63

Spread out your funds 63

Build customer loyalty 64

Get publicity 64

Professional and community associations 65

Get others to promote your business 66

Social marketing 67

Direct marketing 67

Blogs 68

Multiply yourself 69

Your communications network 70

Résumés and Marketing Materials 73

Cover letters 73

Marketing letters 73

Résumés 77

Comments on the traditional résumé in Sample 3 78

Comments on the traditional résumé in Sample 4 80

The Twenty-first Century Résumé 80

Sample profiles 83

Brochures 86

Websites 88

Getting Organized 90

Networking Dos and Don'ts 91

I'm uncomfortable doing it 92

Promoters and supporters 93

Network with a purpose in mind 94

Networking tips and pointers 94

Characteristics of successful networkers 96

Looking for Work on the Internet 98

What you need to monitor 99

Electronic résumés 100

Online personas 102

Finding work via social media sites 103

4 Getting Started   107

Payback Time   107

   Pre-selling tasks   108

   Start your engines   110

   Fine-tune your approach   111

   Final thoughts   111

   Get regular exercise   111

   Keep mentally fit   112

   Polish your communication skills   112

   Continue to grow   112

   Take some risks   112

   Say no more often   112

   Try looking back   113

   Be kind to yourself   113

5 Guidelines for Post-Secondary Students   115

Getting Ready   115

   Overview   115

   Common mistakes by students   116

   Essential skills for students   118

   You and the Internet   122

   Creating a financial plan   123

   Action plan   124

   Sample marketing letter for grads   127

   Sample twenty-first century résumé for grads   129

   Sample brochure for grads   129

   Sample website for grads   132

6 Career Counselling in Secondary Schools   135

Twenty-first Century Career Counselling   135

   The fourth R   136

   Work centers   137

Co-op education 138
Building alliances 139
Marketing tools for students 140
Sample marketing letter for students 141
Sample envelope 143
Sample cover letter for students 144
Sample twenty-first century résumé for students 146
Sample brochure for students 148
Sample website for students 148
Things to Think About 151
Official unemployment statistics 153
Secondary and post-secondary education 154
The road ahead 155

7 Managing Your Career 157

Career Management 157
Become career fit 159
Manage your career 159
Sharpen your communication skills 160
Get connected 160
Stay current 161
Expand and cultivate your network 161
Review your finances 161
Take care of yourself 163
Become You Inc. 164
Establish you inc. 164
Loyalty 165
Outsourcing 165
Increase your employability 166
Selling you inc. 166
The foundation 167
Effective selling 167

Can you help them? 168

Pick your brain 168

Test you 168

Show your stuff 169

Objections 169

Pricing 170

Resilience 170

Appendix 173

Answers to Quiz 1: The Workplace 173

Answers to Quiz 2: You, the Brand 177

Answers to Quiz 3: Networking 179

Quizzes

1. The Workplace 23

2. You, the Brand 72

3. Networking 97

Checklists

1. Preparation 55

2. Marketing 106

Samples

1. Cover Letter 74

2. Marketing Letter 76

3. Traditional Résumé Example 1 79

4. Traditional Résumé Example 2 81

5. Twenty-first Century Résumé 84

6. Brochure 87

7. Website 89

8. Weekly Action Plan 91

9. Electronic Résumé 101

10. Marketing Letter for Grads 128

11. Twenty-first Century Résumé for Grads 130

12. Brochure for Grads   131

13. Website for Grads   133

14. Marketing Letter for Students   142

15. Envelope   144

16. Cover Letter for Students   145

17. Twenty-first Century Résumé for Students   147

18. Brochure for Students   149

19. Website for Students   150

For Jennifer

Until one is committed, there is hesitancy, the chance to draw back, always ineffectiveness, concerning all acts of initiative and creation.

There is one elementary truth the ignorance of which kills countless ideas and splendid plans: that the moment one definitely commits oneself, then Providence moves too.

All sorts of things occur to help one that otherwise would never have occurred.

A whole stream of events issues from the decision, raising in one's favor all manner of unforeseen incidents and meetings and material assistance which no man could have dreamed would have come his way.

Whatever you can do or dream you can, begin it. Boldness has genius, power and magic in it.

Begin it now.

— Johann Wolfgang von Goethe

PREFACE

We're a society that knows how to apply for a job. The challenge for employment seekers today is to become proficient at finding work. That's a much more complicated process than applying for a job.

— *Ron McGowan*

The vast majority of employment seekers, be they college/university graduates or experienced people who are losing their jobs, have no idea about how to find work. Like most of society, they're stuck in the twentieth century and focus, almost exclusively, on finding a traditional job. Those jobs, which have been the mainstay of our economy for over 100 years, are in decline, yet our society, governments, and institutions are still structured as if they were the norm. In trend-setting California, according to a study by the University of San Francisco, only about 30 percent of the workforce have traditional jobs. This reality is where we're all headed — and we're not ready for it.

Like it or not, employment seekers need to face the reality of today's workplace and be willing to accept temporary or contract work without reservations. They also need to accept the fact that there's no guarantee that anyone will offer them employment. They may need to create their own employment. That doesn't mean they have to give up looking for a job, if that's what they want; it means recognizing how the workplace has changed and understanding that the path to a traditional job today is often via the temporary or contract work route. Today it makes more sense to look for work as opposed to looking for a job. But that is a huge psychological shift for people to make in their approach to finding employment considering how entrenched the traditional full-time-job model continues to be in our society.

Today's employment seeker must be more entrepreneurial and enterprising in his or her search for work than previous generations, and needs to be better at selling themselves. Acquiring self-marketing skills is a must as is the ability to find hidden employment opportunities, since at least 80 percent of the employment opportunities today are never advertised. Finally, employment seekers need to learn how to approach employers in a strategically effective way rather than the reactive, mostly passive approach used by people in the twentieth century.

Misleading Unemployment Statistics

The official unemployment statistics published by governments in western countries are a sham. They don't come close to measuring the true state of unemployment. A *New York Times* article on April 12, 2008, under the heading "Many More Are Jobless Than Are Unemployed" compares the unemployment rate with the jobless rate. It points out that the unemployment rate only includes people without jobs who are actively looking for work, whereas the jobless rate counts the proportion of people without jobs with the qualifier that some of these do not want to work. At the time of the article, the official unemployment rate was 4.1 percent and the jobless rate was 13.1 percent. The true rate of unemployment is somewhere between these numbers.

Part-time work and full-time work are often combined in reporting the number of jobs being created which can give a misleading reading on the health of the economy. An example of this was given in a June 7, 2008 Canwest News Service article on Canada's job growth, considered to be pretty robust at that time. It pointed out that in the year prior to the article, part-time employment had risen at nearly twice the gains in full-time jobs. The headline statistic for the previous month had shown that there was job growth in Canada, which on the surface was true. But that growth was derived from a gain of forty thousand part-time jobs and a loss of thirty-two thousand full-time jobs.

In a series of articles in February 2005 in Scotland's *Sunday Herald* newspaper that looked at how unemployment statistics are produced there, a Glasgow University lecturer who studies this area commented that "This country is very good at hiding large chunks of the unemployed through statistics." *The Economist* magazine ran a feature in September 2006 on Sweden. As part of the coverage on what was going on there it stated that "Sweden is a world champion at massaging its' jobless figures." Irish unemployment hit a 9-year high of 5.9 percent according to an Associated Press report on July 30, 2008. The Fine Gael party suggested the figures would be much worse were it not for the large number of Eastern Europeans who were leaving the country to head home because of the weak job market in Ireland.

Kidding ourselves that the employment situation is better than it actually is, is the worst position we could take in dealing effectively with the challenges in today's workplace. Unfortunately, that is exactly what we are doing. We need to overhaul the methodologies we use to produce our monthly unemployment statistics, because they are giving us a false reading. We must expand our approach to this area. We need to know how many people are underemployed, including all the college/university grads and qualified, downsized workers who can't find decent jobs and who are working in service jobs to make ends meet. We need to know how many people have given up looking for work because they can't find a decent job, estimated to be over 3 million in the United States alone. And we need to focus on the quality of work that people are engaged in, and less on the simplistic approach that tells us that x percentage of the workforce is employed. How many are working for minimum wage? How many are working part-time? How many have temporary work? How many are contract workers? How many are self employed?

Challenges for Educators

The fundamental challenge for colleges and universities is that for generations they've been turning out employees. Now, increasingly, they will need to turn out entrepreneurs, or students who have an enterprising approach to finding work. This doesn't mean students have to start a business when they graduate, though those who want to do this should be encouraged and given as much help as possible to succeed. It does mean that graduates must have an entrepreneurial mentality in terms of marketing themselves and meeting the needs of employers. We tend to equate anything related to entrepreneurship to be the domain of business/commerce and MBA students. We need to change that thinking and recognize that this also applies to graduates in the liberal arts, social sciences, and every other sector in post-secondary education. Like all other employment seekers, today's graduates must acquire self-marketing skills and be right on top of what is happening in the sectors they want to work in. The key question is, who is going to teach them these skills?

The biggest weakness in the post-secondary education sector in all countries is the lack of experience in today's workplace by those who are responsible for education policy, funding, administration, and delivery. How do these people who live in the land of the steady paycheck and traditional benefits relate to the challenges graduates face who will make their living from contract, temporary, and part-time employment with few, if any benefits, including a pension?

There's a huge disconnect between these bureaucrats, administrators, and educators and their students in terms of their own work environment and the workplace their students are entering. And that disconnect will exist into the foreseeable future.

Going forward, we must find ways to educate those already in the education system about the challenges of earning a living in today's workplace and hire people at all levels that have this type of experience. Only then can we realistically align the educational system with the needs of today's graduates.

The area of career counselling needs a major overhaul and more resources need to be allocated to it. This area has never been a high priority within the education system, and that has to change. While there are a few examples of innovative thinking in this area, in the main, most colleges and universities are doing a poor job of preparing their students for today's workplace. And some of the career counsellors who do recognize the need to update and improve the services they offer to their students are not getting the resources they need or the support of senior administrators.

Effective career counselling must be a part of the curriculum, not an option, as it currently is. Before they can graduate, all students must be required to take workshops and courses provided by the career counselling department that educate them about today's workplace and shows them how to succeed in it. However, that is based on the assumption that the people who are teaching these workshops and courses are themselves experienced in today's workplace and have earned a living outside of the twentieth century, traditional, full-time-job model. We also need people in these departments who are entrepreneurial, have operated their own businesses, and who can adequately prepare students who want to pursue that option.

A New Era

Our ancestors must be having a good laugh as they watch us struggle to wean ourselves off the traditional, twentieth century job. If you look at your family tree, you're likely to see that you're descended from self-employed people who earned their living as contractors, tradespeople, craftspeople, and small-business owners.

When the concept of full-time employment working for someone else became widespread with industrialization, many of our forefathers thought it was a crazy idea. It was seen as unpleasant, unnatural, and an inhuman way to work. It's the ultimate irony. The job, that thing that our ancestors saw as abhorrent, is the thing to which we've become addicted.

The workplace is currently going through one of the most significant changes to occur in the past hundred years. But it's a mixed bag. While many workers are facing real hardships in trying to cope with these changes, others are sailing along virtually untouched by them.

There is work available, but a lot of it is not packaged in the form of a job, as we traditionally understand that term. The onus is on those looking for work to find the employment opportunities that are out there, or in some cases, to create their own. This is a new role for most people, and our education, training, and in some cases our upbringing does not prepare us well for it.

Those who are unable or unwilling to adapt to this reality will find themselves competing for a dwindling number of conventional, full-time jobs. Those who aren't afraid of a freelance career, who can adapt their job-search strategies and market themselves effectively, will have more options, offer more value to employers, and best position themselves for twenty-first century success.

In This Edition

Throughout this edition you will find updated commentary and insights on key happenings in today's workplace and where informed professionals are suggesting it is headed. College/university students, graduates, and experienced people who have lost their jobs don't have the luxury of waiting for governments or the education system to catch up with the needs of employment seekers in the twenty-first century. They need to take ownership of this issue themselves as do people who are underemployed or who want to prepare themselves for the possibility of losing their jobs.

Thousands of graduates and experienced people in the US, Canada, the UK, and Ireland have already benefited from the earlier editions of this book. It provides a blueprint for finding employment opportunities in a strategically effective way. This book doesn't provide any easy answers. There are none. But for those who are prepared to do all the work required in this book and who are also prepared to move out of their comfort zone and take some chances, the payoff will be that they will be miles ahead of the average employment seeker. And they will be on a solid foundation to succeed regardless of the upcoming challenges in the workplace.

INTRODUCTION

There's a lot of confusion, ignorance, and denial going on in society's attitude towards today's workplace. For people who are losing their jobs, or college/university students about to enter the workplace, accepting the reality of what is going on is difficult. For several generations the foundation of most peoples' economic stability has been a steady job. Notwithstanding the fact that millions of people have been losing those jobs for several decades, the idea of having to earn a living in other, far less predictable ways is very disconcerting to many people. The transitions occurring in the workplace today are among the most significant since the high unemployment of the Great Depression.

Disappearing Benefits

When you come from several generations who took for granted that their job automatically included things like a health benefit package and a pension on retirement, the idea of accepting the fact that these will no longer be included with your job is scary stuff. The cost of having to provide for these things yourself has a major impact on your standard of living and how you will survive when your working days are over.

Some companies are eliminating benefits entirely. Some are offering health benefits but no pension. In the United Kingdom, 80 percent of the companies with pension plans have closed that option to new employees. Even in large successful companies like IBM, Motorola, and Lockheed Martin, a traditional company pension plan is no longer part of the compensation for new employees. In Canada in 2006, 38 percent of employees had a registered employer pension plan according to a Canwest News Service report on July 4, 2008. In Ireland, 54 percent of the workers have pensions, according to a report in *Business Plus* Magazine, September 3, 2008.

You can see how much the workplace has changed in some of the agreements that unions and employers are signing today. Unions now commonly agree to cutbacks in benefits and even wages in return for some job security for their members. This would never have been acceptable as recently as ten years ago.

It's not that the union representatives are any less concerned about the welfare of their members than they have been historically; it's more a question of them facing up to the reality of what is going on in the workplace today.

Facing the truth

Adding to the anxiety and confusion about the workplace are the empty promises being made by some politicians that, in their eagerness to get elected, are playing on peoples' fears. Some suggest that they will reverse the outflow of good paying steady jobs to countries like India and China. Their promises are always presented in very general terms with no specific plans to back them up. Their promises lack specifics because they're not going to happen. Combine this with the misleading, official unemployment numbers we are being fed by governments and it's understandable why people are confused.

In many respects, we're now a two-tiered society: those who have a traditional job and all the benefits that come with it, and those who are earning a living in non-traditional ways. There's a huge disconnect between those who have had steady jobs for years and those who are looking for work today. And the reality of today's workplace comes as a major shock to people who have lost long-term jobs because of downsizing or because of their employers going bankrupt.

It is in everyone's self-interest to confront the reality of today's (and tomorrow's) workplace and that is largely what this book is all about. It will raise people's awareness of what is going on in the workplace, show them how to find hidden work opportunities, and explain how to make the best of the employment options outside of the traditional job.

In this new era, it's not a question of having a traditional job or not. The reality for an increasing number of workers will be that they earn their living sometimes from a traditional job and at other times from other forms of work. And moving back and forth between these two areas will become commonplace.

How This Book is Organized

To show you how to cope with that reality and how to succeed in the workplace, the book is broken down into the following sections:

Chapter 1: How the workplace has changed

Before you can succeed in today's workplace, you have to understand how it works. It's not the same place that your parents or grandparents worked in, and your approach to being successful in it will have to be different from theirs.

You have to understand the difference between looking for work and applying for a job. Unlike yesterday's workplace, you won't find work in your local newspaper unless you get lucky. Your approach has to be very focused, and you have to learn how to make it easy for employers to hire you. Finally, you have to become adept at self-promotion by being very clear on what you have to offer and how that benefits potential employers.

There are many misconceptions around the idea of contract work. One of the more ironic of these is that some of the people who want to find a stable job think that by taking on contract work, they will be cutting themselves off from finding that job when, in fact, the opposite is true. Contracting offers flexibility and advantages to both the employer and the contractor, and these will be explored.

You need to unload some of your historical notions about how to earn a living and broaden your understanding about what is going on in the workplace. Why is it that some people are constantly in demand while others with equally marketable skills are spinning their wheels?

Chapter 2: What exactly do you have to offer?

Knowing yourself and what you have to offer potential employers takes on a whole new dimension in today's workplace. It's no longer enough to identify yourself as an accountant, graphic designer, librarian, or whatever; you have to identify the specific skills that you have to offer and how those benefit the employer you want to work with.

For most people, before they move forward, they need to take a step backward and take some time to analyze and identify the things that are important to them in their lives and in their careers. Many people make the mistake of rushing from one job or contract to another before they have even defined the type of work that makes sense for them and the type of companies that they would enjoy working with.

This phase is critical if you want to succeed in the workplace of the twenty-first century, but unfortunately it is one of the most neglected areas in defining effective career strategies. That's because it's not easy and it may be uncomfortable for you, but it's the foundation on which every other aspect of being successful in today's workplace is built.

Chapter 3: How to market yourself

Today's workplace demands that you become adept at marketing yourself, otherwise you will miss out on work opportunities or be bypassed by less qualified people who are doing a better job of marketing themselves than you are. The myths around selling yourself will be dispelled, and you will be given strategies and tools for selling yourself that will make the experience more effective and therefore more enjoyable and gratifying.

You know more about selling than you think you do, and most people have false notions about how to successfully sell themselves. Many people are uncomfortable with this area, and the reasons for that will be explored. You'll be pleasantly surprised at how effective you can be at selling yourself once you understand how the process works.

Chapter 4: Getting started

This section lays out the steps you have to take to begin to earn your living outside of a traditional job, and it provides strategies for increasing your chances of finding work. These strategies will increase your effectiveness and reduce the frustration that comes from an unfocused approach.

Chapter 5: Guidelines for post-secondary students

College/university students who are about to enter the workplace need to prepare themselves by being very cognizant of the changes going on in it. In this section, they will be given an action plan showing them how to market themselves with an objective of finding work before they graduate. They will also be given sample marketing tools specifically designed for college/university students.

Chapter 6: Career counselling in secondary schools

The place to begin preparing students for success in today's workplace is in our secondary schools. This section provides secondary school career counsellors with ideas on how to raise students' awareness of what is going on in today's workplace and what they should expect when they enter it.

The section includes sample marketing tools specifically designed for secondary school students. These can serve as examples for students to follow in creating their own marketing tools.

Chapter 7: Managing your career

Taking charge of managing your career is something that you must pay more attention to in today's workplace. In the past, your employer may have done this for you as part of the package that came with having a traditional job. Now, whether you have a traditional job, or if you are a contract worker, it is in your own interest to take responsibility for this area.

This chapter will outline what you have to do to successfully manage your career. It also focuses on changes going on in today's workplace that affect your career and personal life.

1
HOW THE WORKPLACE HAS CHANGED

A ship in port is safe, but that's not what ships are built for.

— Ralph Waldo Emerson

Looking for Work Instead of a Job
Is that all there is?

We have lived with the modern concept of a job for so long that we tend to think it has been around forever. In fact, it was introduced to the world about 150 to 200 years ago as nations began to industrialize. Before that, people earned a living by performing a variety of tasks, mostly in agriculture, in areas that were affected by the seasons, the weather, and the time of day. When the concept of a job was introduced to society back then, it caused just as much angst among our ancestors as it is causing now that it is in decline.

We also tend to assume, because it is the way the majority of people have earned their living for generations, that a job is the only way to earn a living. In fact, a significant percentage of the workforce doesn't earn their living from traditional jobs. Take the construction industry, for example. For people employed there, their job is tied directly to the project that they're currently building, and when it is

1

finished, so is their job and they have to look for another project. The same could be said for people employed in the arts. If, for example, you're an actor in a movie or a stage show, once the movie or show is over, so is your job and you move on to the next project. This is also true for musicians and other people employed in the arts.

So the idea of your job being tied to the project that you're currently working on is far from new. What's new is that more people who have always had a traditional job are finding that their livelihood is now going to be earned this way. What is disconcerting is that most of us come from a background where our parents and grandparents made their living from a traditional job, which, for the most part, meant that their careers were stable and they had some security. Most of us still long for that security, but it's getting harder to come by.

The rise of the temporary or contingent worker

The twentieth century was the century of mass production and large corporations, and the workplace was dominated by industrial giants like General Motors. At the end of the century, the biggest employer in the United States was Manpower, a company that specializes in temporary and contingent workers.

In the manufacturing sector, one of the improvements that companies have made to make their process more efficient and economic is to employ a just-in-time approach to the inventory of parts that they carry. Instead of having large quantities of these parts sitting in inventory for long periods before they get used up, they access those parts from their suppliers at the time that they are needed in the manufacturing process and have thus eliminated the need for costly inventories.

The same type of thing is happening in the workplace as companies increasingly view the work to be done in terms of projects and think of their staffing needs in terms of what they need for current and upcoming projects. The idea of a temp, or temporary worker, has been around for decades, but it tended to be restricted to clerical and office staff like receptionists and data entry clerks. Now companies are hiring temporary workers at all levels within the organization.

This is particularly true in the Information Technology or IT sector. That industry is very project oriented, and IT companies regularly hire people for projects with no expectation that their employment will become long-term. Even in Japan, the last bastion of the idea of lifetime employment, many companies where employees have traditionally expected to spend their entire careers with that company are now moving towards hiring temporary workers.

A January 5, 2008 article in *The Economist* titled "Sayonara, salaryman" points out that almost 40 percent of the workforce in Japan are part-time, contingent, and contract workers and that this category is growing while those with permanent jobs is decreasing. It also points out that today's young workers are not interested in accepting the corporate paternalism of their parents' generation where work was the center of their lives and even led in some cases to "karoshi" or "death by overwork."

Outsourcing

"The unearned advantages of having been born as Canadians or Americans may be about to evaporate." This interesting perspective from management expert Tom Peters — writing in *Maclean's* (December 1, 2003) on the issue of outsourcing — applies to all western countries, not only Canada and the United States. What he is suggesting may evaporate are jobs that we have taken for granted for decades, along with a lifestyle and standard of living that have been the envy of many people who live outside of western countries. Many thousands of these jobs, particularly in manufacturing and in the IT sector, have already evaporated and moved overseas.

Dan Pink, in his excellent book *A Whole New Mind,* says that "outsourcing is overhyped in the short term. But it's underhyped in the long term." That opinion is supported by experts' predictions of the number of jobs that will move overseas from western countries to countries like India and China in the next few years and beyond. So far manufacturing and the IT sector have lost the most jobs, and those losses are expected to continue. But these job losses may be the canary in the coal mine. Most experts are predicting that the next wave of jobs moving overseas will be in the insurance, financial services, customer support, and engineering sectors.

It's not just a question of jobs in western countries moving overseas. Foreign multinationals are aggressively going after markets in western countries, taking on the local multinationals on their own turf. A July 31, 2006, article in *BusinessWeek* cites the example of

China's Huawei Technologies Co., which won a huge contract with British Telecommunications PLC in a deal that "sent a chill through the rest of the telecom manufacturers."

The same article states that over the next decade, the World Bank projects that developing nations' share of world gross domestic product is expected to grow from one-fifth to one-third.

Ron Hira is considered one of the leading experts in this area and has written a book titled *Outsourcing America: What's Behind Our National Crisis and How We Can Reclaim American Jobs.* In a July 3, 2005 interview published in *The New York Times,* he was asked in regard to outsourcing, "How can this trend be stopped?"

His answer was "There's nothing that can be done to stop it. The question is, how do we adapt to it and deal with the negative effects?"

That answer should be a wake-up call to governments and business leaders in western countries.

Michigan governor Jennifer Granholm's response to outsourcing is a plan to make her state the innovation capital of the United States. As the historical US hub of automobile manufacturing, Michigan has lost thousands of jobs to outsourcing in the past couple of decades. In July 2006 Google announced plans to open a Michigan operation that will generate 1,000 direct jobs and 1,200 indirect jobs over 5 years. Michigan is offering Google tax breaks over the next 20 years as an incentive for creating these jobs.

When General Motors can get their cars built in China for $2 an hour versus $34 an hour in the US, you don't need a degree in economics to understand why they are now the biggest foreign car manufacturer in China. This is also an example of why manufacturing jobs, which have been a key part of the economies in western countries for decades, will continue to move overseas.

Dan Pink points out that the conventional view thirty years ago was that an economy couldn't be based on services — manufacturing had to be the foundation. When asked how the US can survive outsourcing, he suggested, "We massively underestimate human ingenuity and resilience."

The future, he says, will bring "industries we can't imagine and jobs which we lack the vocabulary to describe."

Our future, in other words, lies in our imagination — to create products and services that the world doesn't know it is missing. Dan makes a valid point but unless we pay more attention to the impact outsourcing is having on our workforce and find ways to deal with its negative effects, as Ron Hira suggests, we're in danger of becoming nations of Wal-Mart and Starbucks employees.

A new relationship

An employee with a company in yesterday's workplace could safely assume that included with their job were a variety of benefits and services that the employer would supply. Benefits ranged from dental plans to pension plans, and you could often expect the employer to assume the responsibility for such things as mapping out a career plan for you.

Even your employability and expectation of being with the company on a long-term basis was a given once you had gone through the hiring process and had landed a full-time job. Today, having a full-time job is no guarantee that your future with the company is assured. Your security is tied to the value that the company perceives you to bring to their operation at any given time.

More companies are looking at employees as commodities, i.e., we will pay you for the set of skills that you bring to us but benefit packages, career planning, continuing education, upgrading of skills, and those types of issues are viewed as costly overhead, and the onus to provide for them has shifted from the company to the employee.

The consensus among the experts on the workplace is that today everybody is a temporary worker and the only security you can expect is in having a set of current, marketable skills that are in demand.

The shift to smaller companies

The workplace of the twentieth century, up until about the 1970s, was dominated by large companies. This changed in the 1980s and '90s to the point where, for years now, the vast majority of jobs and work opportunities are created by small businesses. Small today could mean a single operator who has expanded to the point where he or she needs an extra body on a full-time or part-time basis.

This shift has many repercussions for today's workers, especially those who have lost their jobs with a medium to large, well-established company. Whether the shift is positive or negative is all over the map depending on how informed the individual is about the workplace and how well they've positioned themselves to survive in it.

Many of today's small business owners were formerly full-time employees in large companies who decided that self-employment made more sense for them than looking for another full-time job. Also, more young people coming out of college or university are starting their own businesses than at any other time in the past. According to a May 2005 Ipsos-Reid poll, 40 percent of Canadian college and university students would like to be their own bosses by becoming entrepreneurs or consultants.

In the US, according to a *New York Times* article on May 1, 2008, over 2,000 colleges and universities are now offering courses in entrepreneurship, up from 253 institutions offering these courses in 1985. The article also pointed out that many colleges have turned to active or retired business owners rather than academics to teach these courses. It also pointed out that some people see a strong liberal arts education as a foundation for success in these courses and that entrepreneurship in business schools is often too narrowly focused.

A new set of expectations

While there are no hard and fast rules that define how small and large businesses operate, there are some things that you generally can count on to be different between them. If you lost a job with a large company, you've lived in a world where you could expect that your job included a decent benefit package, paid overtime, a nice office, and other perks that you probably took for granted. If you expect to find all or most of these things when you join a small company, you're probably going to be disappointed. You may also be disappointed if you expect to earn the same salary as you did in the past.

The president or owner or the principals of the company, who often risk everything they have to establish it, may not have many of the things that you may feel you're entitled to, like security, benefits packages, and so on, so it's unrealistic for you to expect to have them.

You'll probably wear more hats in your job than you have in the past, and you could be much more involved in the important decision-making processes affecting where the company is going. You may have an opportunity to pick up some stock options if the company is planning to go public. You may become a telecommuter and perform most of your work from home and be expected to supply or help to purchase the PC that you need to do this. You may be a contract worker with no benefits included in your compensation and no buy-out or golden handshake at the end of your employment even if you've worked with the company for years.

You may have opportunities to advance your career — a thing that may never have happened with a large company. Your contributions could have much more influence over the success or failure of the company. You may be expected to provide leadership in guiding the company in new directions, and that could be a new role for you.

No more entitlements

If you're over 40 or have been strongly influenced by your parents' experience in the workplace, you may need to make some significant and fundamental changes in your thinking about your career and what to expect in your working life. In yesterday's workplace, the relationship between the worker and the employer was much more paternalistic than it is today.

The reason why so many people are devastated by the loss of a full-time job often has more to do with other aspects than the financial one. What the individual also loses is a sense of belonging to a community, some dignity and self-respect, pride in what they do, and they often have a sense of betrayal if they feel that they gave the company all that they had to offer. These non-tangible things that come with a job in a large company may not necessarily come with a job in a small company.

How people react to the changes that arise from going from a large to a small company will vary according to how secure they are with themselves, how well they adapt to change, how informed they are about the workplace, and their ability to rise above the day-to-day challenges and view the transition that the workplace is going through from a broader, more philosophical point of view.

A need to take the broader view

As the workplace goes through its current transition, those who have lost their jobs are having a tough time dealing with the realities of the new workplace. In many cases their kids are also looking at them and wondering what they should do to position themselves to earn a decent living. The range of emotions goes from those who feel liberated by the changes going on in the workplace — "good riddance to the traditional job" — is their attitude to those at the other end of the scale, who may be devastated by the loss of their jobs. There's no quick fix to any of this. We'll just have to adjust to these changes, as our ancestors had to adjust to the changes that took place in their lifetimes.

There is work available, but if you're looking for it to come in the shape of a traditional job with all of the benefits and security that we've become accustomed to, you're probably going to be disappointed. Finding the work that's available is also going to be a lot more challenging. For most of us it will require developing new skills, being much more informed about what is going on in society and in the workplace, and finally shedding some long-held attitudes about work, jobs, and expectations.

You're going to have to become more adept at selling yourself and anticipating and understanding the needs of the employer that you want to work with. That's a new role for most of us and it won't come naturally. You'll have to learn how to do it and how to do it in a way that is effective for you.

Facing reality

When the realities of the new workplace are laid out for us, most of us, at a rational level, can relate to them. It's common sense. The big challenge is to psychologically accept that reality and adjust our lives and attitudes towards earning a living. That challenge will continue for the foreseeable future, because in that time frame most people around us will still have traditional jobs. One of the biggest problems facing people who have lost their jobs is looking around and seeing the majority of people they know still working in traditional jobs. This leaves them feeling victimized and lost.

Even though the majority of people are well aware that significant changes are going on in the workplace, they can't really relate to the challenges that people who have lost their jobs are facing. They only get it when it happens to them or someone in their family.

There's denial going on here, of course. Sure, we know about the turmoil going on in the workplace, but if we still have a job, we don't want to think too much about the challenges we would face if we lost that job. It's an attitude that many of us have towards major diseases as well, and it explains why so many people are shattered when they lose their jobs. It's the "it'll never happen to me" syndrome. Our first reaction is to replace the job we lost with another job, and if the prospects for that are bleak, we panic and look at our situation from the worst possible point of view.

At some point, however, we have to face the realities of the new workplace, and one of the fundamental changes that we have to make in our attitude is to recognize the fact that there is work out there just not necessarily jobs. We have to learn to cope with the new realities and adjust our approach to looking for work accordingly. That doesn't mean giving up looking for a job, if that's what is important to you. It means that you have to accept the fact that the route to finding that job will be different from what it has been in the past.

It's not all bad

We should also try to be as objective as possible about the changes going on in the workplace. Some people have actually benefited from losing their jobs in that it has forced them to go through some soul-searching about what is important to them in their careers and they have come out of the process happier for the experience. They find out that the job they were so attached to was a bad fit for them and that there are other, more attractive options and ways to make a living that make sense for them.

Some people who get involved as contractors, initially with skepticism and trepidation, find that as they gain confidence and realize that they can earn a living this way, they wouldn't go back to a traditional job if it was offered to them. People who have just lost their job may have difficulty believing that, but if they take the time to talk to people who have made the transition to contracting, and they should make a point of doing that, they will find that there is a world beyond that of the traditional job.

An example of the struggle people continue to have in accepting contract work was given in an October 24, 2006 article on Workopolis, Canada's biggest job site. A worker in the auto sector who had lost his job and was having no success in finding another job after months of searching was seeking advice. He had just been offered a four-month contract by a company he respected in the auto sector and his question was; should he accept it or continue to seek "real" employment?

It's just possible that once we work our way through the transition that is currently going on in the workplace, we will pass on to our children a workplace that is healthier and more fulfilling for them.

Most Employment Opportunities Are Hidden

Where are the opportunities?

Looking for employment opportunities in yesterday's workplace was a fairly straightforward procedure. You looked in the newspaper, called some friends and associates, maybe called a few employment agencies, and checked with your professional association or union. You still need to do these things, but they won't lead you to the majority of the employment opportunities that exist in today's workplace. You need to significantly expand your approach to include:

- Monitoring the websites of companies that you would like to work with and who you feel are likely to be adding to their staff. Most company websites these days have a section where they list their current employment opportunities. In the IT sector, this is the main way in which many companies advertise their jobs or contract opportunities. There's even an attitude on the part of some of these companies that if you can't find these opportunities on your own, they're not interested in you. In other words, they want people who are "with it" and who know how to find employment in their industry.

- Most professional associations have a job-search service which they provide to their members. Companies who want to hire members deal directly with the association, which in turn lists the information on its website. Some industry associations do this as well, and sometimes you can access this information even if you're not a member.

- While most of the major newspapers still include a career or employment section, you may find more opportunities listed online in their electronic employment service, which more and more companies are using instead of listing their requirements in print. Most of these services allow you to post your résumé on their site for free, and some of them will automatically notify you when an opportunity comes up that matches your job specifications. Some of these sites are also a very effective way to monitor what is going on in the workplace and to learn from the experience of others who are actively seeking employment.

- There are lots of online job sites available today, some that are generic and others that specialize in particular professions or geographical areas. One of the biggest online job sites is www.monster.com. Other sites are excellent resources for monitoring workplace activity, trends and news, www.rileyguide.com being one of the best of these.

- Marci Alboher's "Shifting Careers" column in *The New York Times* is also recommended: www.shiftingcareers.blogs.nytimes.com.

We've already learned that the vast majority of employment opportunities are generated by small businesses. These businesses may not have a website at this point and if they do, it may not have a section on employment. In order to flush out these opportunities, you need to access every possible tool.

Finding employment opportunities

Most of the opportunities that exist today never hit the mainstream media or get posted on a website. The ways to find them include:

- Becoming a news hound and staying on top of trends in the workplace and in society. If you find that you are constantly being surprised by events when they are reported in the mainstream media, you're not doing as good a job as you need to of monitoring what's going on.

- You need to create your own database of news sites and job sites and monitor them regularly. Indiscriminate web surfing is not the answer. You need to approach this area in a diligent, intelligent, and creative way to ensure that you know more about what is going on in the workplace than the average person does. Many websites offer free newsletters filled with current news, and you can have them sent to you automatically on a regular basis. For example, if you want to keep abreast of events in the IT sector, www.wired.com is a good site to be connected to.

- There are always seminars, meetings, conventions, trade shows, and courses going on in your community. You need to be monitoring these to make sure that you don't miss out on an event that could be important to you in your search for work opportunities. They also help to keep you informed about what is going on.

- You need to network effectively. There's a whole section devoted to this later in the book, but let's recognize at this point that you must be constantly networking in a creative and effective way. Word of mouth is a pretty low-tech way to advertise in today's world, and many employment opportunities are filled this way.

- Use your imagination and be creative. Maybe the employment opportunity that you're looking for hasn't hatched yet in the mind of the employer who could benefit from using your set of skills. Look for unmet needs, and the better you're connected to what is going on in the workplace and the world, the more likely you are to identify these. Maybe you need to create your own work opportunity by going directly to an employer with an idea whose time has come. Smart contractors and job seekers are doing this all the time.

- Get involved with professional and business organizations, and that means volunteering and being active on the executive level, not casually showing up for an occasional monthly meeting. Also monitoring the websites of professional and business organizations both within and outside of your community is a good way to keep up with what's going on. Most of the chambers of commerce have a website today, and you may pick up some useful news items by monitoring them. Some of them also list their members and the companies the members are with. You could pick up some useful contact names. As long as you approach these people professionally and you are polite, they will probably be willing to give you some information.

- Notwithstanding all of the preceding references to the Internet, do not discount the print media, particularly trade magazines and professional publications. You will find useful information in these that you won't find on the Internet. Most cities have one or two primary publications that focus on business and industry, and if you don't subscribe to these, you should at least monitor them regularly. To get an overview of all of the main business and industry publications, including international publications, look at www.ceoexpress.com on a regular basis.

- Your local library is still a very useful resource for keeping in touch with what is going on, and accessing their services can save you a lot of time. Many libraries offer courses on doing basic research and how to use the Internet as a research tool.

Obviously, looking for work today is radically different from what it used to be. Key differences between people who are regularly employed and those who are struggling is how well they are informed about what is going on and how systematically they monitor workplace issues and trends.

Why Contracting Makes Sense

Myths about contracting

As noted earlier, one of the most ironic perceptions about working as a contractor is that if you choose to go in this direction, you are cutting yourself off from the possibilty of finding a permanent job. Nothing could be further from the truth. By being active as a contractor, you're adding to your experience and expanding your network of contacts. You'll feel better about yourself since you're actively employed as opposed to sitting on the sidelines waiting for a permanent job to come up, and if one does come up, you can take it.

The basis for this attitude is psychological. If you have earned your living for years by being employed in one or more permanent jobs and that's how your parents and grandparents earned their living, it's a challenge to accept the fact that you can earn a living as a contractor, given the unpredictability of such work versus a permanent job. If you've lived with the security of a paycheck being deposited to your bank account every two weeks throughout your career it's not easy to make the adjustment to contracting, where your earnings are far less predictable. Some people are so addicted to this stable way of living they have difficulty accepting the fact that you can earn a living any other way.

There tends to be a generation gap on this issue too. Younger people who are entering the workforce are more likely to adapt to contracting than their parents are. Since they haven't had the experience of years of getting a steady paycheck, they will adapt more readily to contracting. They're also less likely to be carrying around the emotional baggage that their parents are as they try to adjust to the significant changes that are taking place in the workplace.

It would be wrong to assume, however, that young people are not challenged by the prospect of earning their living as contractors. They are influenced by their parents' attitudes and society's addiction to a job as the only way to earn a living. Our education system doesn't prepare them well for the entrepreneurial option. They may also want the material benefits that come from having a permanent job: a house, a nice car, and a comfortable lifestyle.

Because the concept of earning a living from having a permanent job is still very much a part of the fabric of the society that we live in, contracting tends to be seen as an inferior way to make a living. The fact is that some contractors are much better off than their counterparts who still have permanent jobs. They're earning more and keeping more of what they earn because of the tax advantages that go with contracting. They control when they go on vacation and how often they do it. They have much more freedom in how they work. They're not locked into a nine-to-five, Monday-to-Friday work schedule, and they're more likely to work from home and spend less time commuting, which can be a major stress factor for people who live in cities. While it's true that some contractors, especially those who are new to it, are struggling, many others love what they do and would never go back to the lifestyle imposed by a permanent job.

Working as a contractor is rightfully seen as a form of owning your own business, and that's what scares and makes some people uncomfortable with it. Not everyone sees themselves as an entrepreneur, even though most of our ancestors were self-employed before the modern concept of a job came along. But contracting is a more flexible form of earning a living that can give you the option of switching to a permanent job if one comes up, or staying with contracting if that is your preference. And it's not a life sentence. Even if you currently choose contracting because you love it, you can always change your mind in the future and opt for a permanent job if one is offered to you.

According to a 2005 report from the Global Entrepreneurship Monitor, Ireland is one of the leading countries in Europe in terms of entrepreneurship. Almost 70 percent of the population considers entrepreneurship to be a good career choice. A January 17, 2008 article in *The New York Times* notes that Ireland ranks third in the European Union in early-stage entrepreneurial activity.

Europe's labour market is considered overly rigid, and the countries with the most rigid "job protection" rules also have the highest levels of unemployment. This is the opinion of Ann Mettler, executive director of the Lisbon Council, which is committed to raising European competitiveness.

France is losing many of its young entrepreneurs because of the cultural attitude towards capitalism. A March 11, 2008 article in *The New York Times* points out that an estimated half a million French entrepreneurs, most of them under 35, have left France and moved to the south of England to start up their own business.

What employers are looking for

Looked at from the perspective of employers, and remembering that typically means small businesses today, contracting gives them the flexibility that is often a key factor in their decision to add another body or not.

It's a sad fact that some people are cutting themselves off from finding work by being so inflexible in how they approach employers. They may have a set of skills that the employer can use, but if the only option they are giving the employer is to hire them on a permanent basis, they may be shooting themselves in the foot.

If, on the other hand, they approach the employer on the basis of "Here is the set of skills that I can offer you. Let's see how I could apply them to the projects that you're currently working on and are about to start, " they've just given that employer a whole different set of options for hiring them. Just as the idea of accepting anything other than a permanent job scares some people, the opposite is true for the employer. They're scared of committing to adding to the overhead costs of their operation by hiring a permanent employee when the only business they can count on, are current and upcoming projects. That may only be a guarantee of six months' or a year's work and under those circumstances, which are common in today's workplace, it makes no sense to them to add a permanent employee to their staff.

Employers must also consider the attitude of the person who is looking for work. If that person can't accept anything other than a permanent job, the message they're sending out, often without being aware of it, is hire me and look after me, and that's the last thing that a small business owner wants. They need self-starters who understand the uncertainty in today's workplace and who are willing to share in the risk associated with operating in that environment.

Make It Easy to Get Hired

The number one criteria that today's employer will use in deciding whether or not to hire an additional employee is, will this person add value to my operation and make my life easier? If you understand that and approach the employer in a way that is centered on it, you've significantly increased your chances of being hired versus someone whose approach is still attuned to yesterday's workplace.

The way you communicate; your cover letter, résumé, brochure, and all the other print and electronic marketing tools you are using have all got to be focused on this issue, and that will be a major factor in determining how successful you are in finding work. If you get the employer's attention and determine that indeed they could use your set of skills and let's say that potentially there's an opportunity for a six-month contract, make their decision even easier by suggesting that you ease your way into the contract, say one month at a time, rather than locking them into committing to the whole six months at the outset.

If the opportunity is for a long-term contract and you're excited about working with the company and you have no doubt that you can help them, you may even consider offering to work for them for a week for free to show them what you can do. Smart contractors have landed lucrative contracts by using this approach.

Guess who gets offered the job?

We've identified the fact that in today's workplace most of the work opportunities are hidden. One reason for this is that when companies decide that they want to make a permanent addition to their staff, the first place they will look to is their pool of contract workers, if that makes up part of their workforce. This makes sense since they know those people and what they can do and they in turn know the company.

If people who are looking for work and who are only comfortable with a permanent job understood this, they would be much more inclined to consider contract work as a viable route to finding more permanent work.

Employee referral programs

Employee Referral Programs (ERPs), whereby current employees refer suitable candidates for in-house job opportunities, are becoming increasingly popular with employers, some of whom are meeting up to 60 percent of their hiring needs this way. In some cases such programs account for almost all of the hiring done.

It is common for employers to offer their employees a cash bonus for people they hire from their referrals. But the cash isn't the only reason employees take part. They feel good about seeing people they know being hired, and they're smart enough to know that it's in their interest to only refer people they know are good and who they feel will fit within the culture of the company.

Hiring on the basis of employee referrals is a smart investment for the employer too, since it reduces the time involved in hiring new people and can substantially reduce the cost of recruiting. For people looking for work, being referred by an existing employee significantly increases the probability of their being hired compared to them approaching the employer on their own.

The growth of ERPs helps to explain why many employment opportunities are never advertised and proves yet again why it is so important to be connected to what is going on in the workplace and to be an effective networker. Some companies are sending college and university graduates they've hired, and who have worked out, back to their alma maters as recruiters. Encouraging employees to be active in alumni associations and networks is also seen as a good way to find new hires.

Trying before buying

Another reason why contract work makes sense for both the employer and those who are looking for work is that it gives both parties a chance to get to know one another before making a more permanent commitment. Our working relationships are the only relationships in our lives that we approach with an attitude of making it a permanent commitment before the parties involved know one another.

You can interview, test, and reference check all you want in considering a potential employee, but experience shows us that it's only after working together for a period of time that either party knows if they are compatible with the other party or not. This is another argument in favor of both sides entering into a contract work arrangement before committing to a more permanent one.

Computer-based job simulation technology is becoming an increasingly popular way for companies to attract and assess potential employees. L'Oreal, for example, uses job simulation scenarios as part of the screening process. According to a 2005 study by Rocket-Hire of New Orleans, close to 20 percent of companies are using this tool, and that percentage is expected to grow.

Such technology also allows potential employees to try on a job to see if it is a right fit for them. Although it is an effective tool to use at the beginning of the hiring/screening process, applicants must still expect to do well in interviews, where companies will assess their personalities and communication skills.

Vocation Vacations is a five-year-old company in Portland, Oregon, that gives people the opportunity to "test drive" their dream jobs. They do this by pairing up the individual with a mentor for a couple of days, during which they get hands-on experience in the field they believe they'd like to work in. Participants pay anywhere from a few hundred dollars to a few thousand to experience life as a race car driver, dog trainer, fashion designer, Broadway producer, or whatever. Vocation Vacations has placed hundreds of people in the US and Britain into these dream job simulations.

The Need for Self-Promotion

Why you have to self-promote

One of the main factors that distinguish people who are succeeding in today's workplace from those who are struggling in it is how well they understand the need for self-promotion and how effective they are at doing it. Some people, especially professionals who are over forty and who have lost their jobs, are really challenged by this. Some of them don't see why they should have to do it; after all, they are professionals, accountants, engineers, etc., and they achieved success in their careers before they lost their job. Surely, they reason, their qualifications and experience speak for themselves.

Another reason for being uncomfortable with self-promotion could be your upbringing or your cultural background. You may see the whole subject as unseemly. Blowing your own horn is something you were taught was undignified, and this attitude may have been reinforced by blowhards that you've come across in your life.

The first thing you need to do is to understand what self-promotion is, in the context of doing it to find work. If you have an aversion to loud, self-aggrandizing people, that's good, because that's the last thing you want to become. Employers are not bullied, schmoozed, or coerced into hiring people; they will be just as turned off by this behavior as you are. On the other hand, they're not mind readers, so you can hardly expect them to determine for themselves what your strengths are and how they may be of value to them.

You need to be aware of another one of those shifts that have occurred in the workplace. In yesterday's world, often your experience and qualifications did speak for themselves, so you could still succeed in looking for work with a fairly passive approach. Also you were probably responding to a newspaper ad where the requirements for getting hired were clearly spelled out. Finally, you were probably applying to a large company that had a personnel or human resources department that had time to assess applications that were not as well prepared as they could be.

That's all changed. Remember, most of the work opportunities today are generated by small companies who don't have personnel or human resources departments. Often this task is handled by someone whose expertise is in another area, and hiring is only one of several hats that they wear.

You will often be applying to companies on speculation that they may need your skills rather than responding to a specific ad that you saw in a newspaper or on the Internet. Under these circumstances, the applications that will get attention are those that are very focused, where the applicant has done some research on the company and their résumé is effectively designed to highlight their strengths and how those can benefit the company.

Communication skills are far more important than they used to be, especially in the area of looking for work. The workplace is a more fast-paced and busy environment than it used to be, and it is more difficult to get an employer's attention. The focus of the communication must be clearly on what you can do for them and not the other way around, and it must be specific and geared to their needs and not be a general description of your past career.

If you are soliciting companies for contract work, maybe you should replace your résumé with a simple brochure, or one of the electronic marketing tools described in Chapter 3 of this book that, again, have as the main focus your strengths and how those can benefit the company.

Managing your own career

Here is another requirement for succeeding in today's workplace that people don't pay enough attention to. You need to be far more cognizant about who you are, what you're good at, and what type of people and companies you want to work with. If you're currently working on a contract, you should have a plan of action for finding your next contract. It's always a juggling act for today's contract worker.

Unless you're one of the lucky ones who still have a stable job and work for a company that provides some help to map out a career strategy for you, you'll have to take ownership of this issue yourself.

Even if you're in a stable job, you should have some kind of plan in place in case you lose it.

You are responsible for managing your own career, and the only security you have is tied directly to how marketable your skills are, how creative you are in finding work, how well you communicate, and how good you are at recognizing opportunities where you can apply your skills.

The first step in managing your own career is to be very clear on what skills you have to sell to potential employers. Most people are weak in this area. Chapter 2 will eliminate that weakness by getting you to go through a series of exercises to determine exactly what it is you have to sell to potential employers. This will set the stage for Chapter 3, which focuses on how to market yourself. You can't sell yourself effectively unless you're crystal clear on what you have to sell. The better the job you do in Chapter 2, the more comfortable you will be with marketing yourself.

Summary

The objective of this chapter was to make you aware of the changes that have occurred in the workplace. You won't be successful in finding work unless you understand these changes and their impact on you. Most people don't understand them and the consequences of that are: If they lose their job, they feel lost, or if they decide to become a contract worker, they don't know how to go about it.

To be successful, you need to understand the workplace and the changes going on in it at a level far beyond that of the average person. If you don't understand it you'll make the same mistakes that most people make, i.e., using an obsolete approach and set of tools to find work, and you'll also be caught off guard when the changes occur. Here's a recap of what has been covered:

- You need to understand the difference between looking for work and applying for a job. There's a lot of work available today; it's just not packaged in the form of a job — as most people understand the term.

- You need to understand that some of the tangible and non-tangible features that were always part of a traditional job are often not included in contract work.

- You must understand that most of the work opportunities that exist today are found in small companies, and if you've spent your career in a large company, you'll have to change your perception as to your role in the small company and what is expected of you.

- Since most of the work opportunities that exist today are hidden, you need to know how to find them.

- You need to know how employers make their hiring decisions and what they are looking for in contract workers.

- You must understand that your success in today's workplace is tied directly to how effective you are at self-promotion and what self-promotion means in the context of looking for work.

A Note About the Quizzes

There are three quizzes in the book. The point of the quizzes is for you to test, on your own, your knowledge of the material you've read in the section preceding the quiz. To determine what you've learned, you must answer the questions in a comprehensive way rather than with short answers. If the question asks for a true or false answer, for example, the question is not merely whether you think the statement is true or false. Ask yourself why you feel it is true or false, and list all of the reasons you can think of to support your answer.

In the Appendix and on the CD included with this book, are answers to the questions so you can compare your responses. Do not be tempted to look at the answers before you have answered the questions as completely as you can. You'll only be short-changing yourself if you do. If you're not sure about the answer, take a stab at it anyway. You're trying to determine what you know and don't know.

If all of your answers are wrong, as unlikely as that may be, that's not a bad thing. You will find out what you don't know and the areas you have to brush up on. That will make your search for work far more effective and increase your chances of making a good impression in an interview.

QUIZ 1: THE WORKPLACE

1. Name some medium-to-large organizations that potentially could use your skill set and explain why you chose them.

2. Name some small (less than ten employees) organizations that you would like to work with and explain why you chose them.

3. Name some projects that are either underway or will soon be started that might provide employment opportunities for you.

4. Your chances of finding work will be directly related to the number of want ads you respond to, the number of recruiting agencies you register with, and the number of résumés or CVs you send out. True or false?

5. Name the three most active sectors in the economies of the cities or regions in which you want to work.

6. What are the key trends in the sectors in which you want to work?

7. Name some influential people in the sectors in which you want to work.

8. Where do the "players" in the sector you want to work in hang out? What associations do they belong to? What networking events are they likely to attend? Identify the trade shows and conferences coming up in the next six months that they are likely to attend.

9. What are the best media sources for keeping you abreast of new developments in the workplace and in particular the areas you're interested in?

10. Name some websites that will keep you informed about the areas in which you want to work.

11. What are the best electronic and/or print newsletters that will keep you informed about the areas in which you want to work?

12. Can you think of an unmet need in the areas in which you want to work that could be an employment opportunity for you?

13. Outsourcing will destroy the workforces of countries in the western world. True or false?

14. You've just joined the association that you know the "players" in your sector belong to. The executive has asked you to fill the vacant "program chair" position and you've accepted. In putting together the program for the coming year, identify three topics that you know will be of interest to the members.

2

WHAT EXACTLY DO YOU HAVE TO OFFER?

Nothing builds self esteem and self confidence like accomplishment.

— *Thomas Carlyle*

What Is Important and Relevant for You?

One of the positive aspects of the transition that the workplace is going through is that more people are being reflective about their careers, both those currently in a career and younger people who are looking at career options. Before the transition started, you could almost guarantee yourself a secure career by acquiring an education or specialized training that led to a job in one of the professions, like accounting or engineering, or in one of the trades, like carpentry or plumbing.

Since that guarantee is no longer a certainty, more people are taking a broader view of their options for earning a living. One example of this is the significant increase in the area of self-employment. To be successful in today's workplace you need to know what your skills and interests are regardless of whether you're starting out or have years of experience.

That means you have to take the time to go through some self-analysis, either on your own or with some professional help, to determine what your skills and interests are. Most people are challenged by this because it's not easy. It will take time to do it properly, and you'll have to go through it several times to get it right.

Taking a long look inside yourself is difficult. Personal reflection is not high on the priority list of some people. "Just get on with life" is their attitude (and forget this airy-fairy, touchy-feely stuff). Middle-aged businesspeople can be especially challenged by personal reflection. Most people think that they know themselves pretty well and can't see the need for this self-analysis.

You can be sure that those who are succeeding in today's workplace and those who will succeed in the future are those who have taken the time to do a good and thorough job in this area. If you try to short-circuit the process or approach it superficially, you'll pay a price. You'll flounder when you get in front of an employer or decision maker because you won't be secure in knowing who you are and what you have to offer and you'll do a lousy job of selling yourself for the same reasons. You're also more likely to end up in a job or engaged in work that's not a good fit for you.

So let's be clear on the importance of this section before we go any further in the book. Like it or not, it's the key to success. It's the foundation upon which all other aspects of your career success depend. If you're not prepared to spend the time it takes to do a good job here, don't bother with the rest of the book; you'll be wasting your time.

Get some help

Don't try to do all of this on your own. Try to engage a mentor or someone who knows you and whose judgement you trust. Since you are going to identify your key strengths and core set of skills, it makes sense to get a second opinion on just what those are. It will also help to verify what types of jobs, work opportunities, and companies are best suited to you.

You may also have a tendency to be too narrow when looking at your options in your career. When considering your key strengths and interests, don't limit yourself to what you have done only in your work; it's important to include your life outside of work too. Your profile should include all of you, not just the part that relates to your work. Think broadly and boldly in looking at your options. Focus on your limitless potential rather than on your limiting past.

According to Herb Greenberg and Patrick Sweeney of the aptitude-testing consultancy firm Caliper Corp., of Princeton, New Jersey, up to 80 percent of people are "misemployed" (in jobs that don't use their strongest aptitudes and interests). They disclosed this fact in their book *Succeed on Your Own Terms* (released in July 2006), based on an analysis of aptitude tests Caliper has given to thousands of managers worldwide over the past forty years. The tests measure dozens of personality attributes, such as assertiveness, ego, empathy, and risk-taking, that indicate the kinds of work people would find naturally interesting and at which they'd be most likely to do well.

Be patient with yourself

Don't expect self-analysis to come easily to you. Take as much time as you need to come up with a profile that you are comfortable with. Include your failures as well as your successes when analyzing your past but keep the failures in perspective. T.J. Watson, the founder of IBM, said, "Success is on the far side of failure." What he meant by this is in order to be successful, you'll have to endure your share of failure. In identifying failures, make sure that you know why things didn't work out the way you expected them to and learn from the experience.

When analyzing the successes in your career, focus on the projects that you worked on and what the payoff was to the company and the people involved. Being clear about the successful projects that you worked on and your role in them will increase your strength and self-confidence. Once you've done a good job in this area, you'll be eager to sell yourself.

You'll know what excites you and what you're good at, and your enthusiasm will come across when you're talking to a potential employer or client. Don't be reticent about your successes. Being successful in selling yourself comes in part from knowing why you were successful in the past and in knowing that you can apply the same skills to help the employer or client that you're talking with.

An ongoing process

You'll never know enough about yourself, your skills, and why people would buy them. You have to keep working at it and polishing your presentation and communication skills. One of the key reasons why people are struggling to find work today is that they are very complacent about identifying their key skills and strengths and consequently they cannot do a good job of selling themselves. It shouldn't come as a surprise that they don't like selling themselves. They haven't done their homework and therefore they are not equipped to sell effectively.

The following exercises will take some time to complete and will require lots of revisions before you come up with answers that you are satisfied and comfortable with, so get yourself a pen and lots of writing paper.

How Career Fit Are You?

If you are "career fit" you should be able to easily answer the following questions:

- What are your top three strengths and talents?
- What environment brings out your best work?
- What were the most satisfying aspects of your past work?
- What are your work values?
- What is your work style?
- How do your skills match your current workplace needs?
- What have you done to upgrade your skills in the past year?
- What career action plans are you currently working on?
- Do you have a written career development plan?

If you couldn't answer these questions comfortably, you need to work on getting into "career shape."

Defining Your Personal and Career Profile
Who are you?

Can you imagine a company that's about to launch a new product line sending their sales force out to see their customers and present that product line before they have given them any training on it? Or an athlete who rarely gives any thought to the strengths and weaknesses of an opponent or team that he or she is about to play? Or an actor who doesn't rehearse before going in front of an audience or performing in a stage show, movie, or television program?

Because they're professionals, they understand that it is imperative that they know exactly what to say or do before they get in front of the customer, opponent or audience. You need to take your cue from these experts in preparing yourself for getting in front of a prospective employer or client. Just like them, the more you practise, rehearse, and train, the greater will be your chances of success when you meet an employer and the more confident you'll be when selling yourself.

The more you understand your successes, abilities, interests, and attitudes, the more comfortable you'll be with yourself. It's also more likely that you will be talking to employers who are a good match for you rather than wasting your time with companies that are incompatible with your goals.

In the first exercise, select from the following list (feel free to add to it) what you consider to be your top five strengths in terms of your personality and character. Then come up with at least two examples of situations where you have shown these strengths. Finally, rank them in terms of their importance to you so that if you were asked in an interview to name your two top strengths, you could easily do so.

Personal Characteristics

Friendly	Good-Natured	Quiet
Adaptable	Helpful	Adventurous
Honest	Realistic	Aggressive
Humorous	Reflective	Ambitious
Reserved	Assertive	Responsible
Kind	Calm	Likeable
Careful	Cautious	Loyal
Sensible	Cheerful	Sensitive
Sincere	Sociable	Competitive
Modest	Confident	Conservative
Optimistic	Consistent	Outgoing
Curious	Patient	Thoughtful
Tough	Discreet	Persuasive
Easygoing	Poised	Understanding
Emotional	Progressive	Witty

Personal Characteristics — My Top Five Strengths

1.

2.

3.

4.

5.

Situations Where I've Shown Them

1.

2.

3.

4.

5.

What are your values?

Who do you admire and respect? Which companies would you like to work for or would you recommend to a friend and what is it about them that you respect? What are the attributes of the ideal types of work that you would like to be involved with in terms of their impact on you, your family and friends and the world you live in? From the following list, select the five most important values that you want to associate with the work that you do or would like to do. Add to the list any values that are not shown but are important to you.

Value	Example
Helping Society	Something that helps to improve the world we live in.
Helping Others	Something that directly helps individuals or groups.
Public Contact	You need lots of this daily.
Work with Others	You need to belong to a group.
Work Alone	You prefer to work on projects on your own.
Competition	You like to test yourself against others.
Make Decisions	You like being in control.

Work under Pressure	You thrive on being continually challenged.
Influence People	You like to have a personal impact on others.
Knowledge	You need to be continually learning.
Work Mastery	You need to be an expert in what you do.
Artistic Creativity	You need freedom to express your talents.
General Creativity	You need to influence how things are done.
Aesthetics	The beauty of things and ideas must be in your work.
Supervision	You like to be responsible for others.
Change and Variety	These must be a part of what you do.
Precision Work	Attention to detail is important to you.
Stability	You like a routine that is predictable.
Security	You must feel that your job is for the long term.
Recognition	You need regular feedback on your worth.
Fast Pace	You need to work in a dynamic environment.
Excitement	You must experience this in your work.
Adventure	There must be some risk inherent in your work.
Financial Gain	Being rewarded financially is very important to you.

Physical Challenge	You need to use your physical abilities in your work.
Independence	You don't want someone looking over your shoulder.
Moral Fulfillment	Your work must meet your moral standards.
Community	You need to participate in community affairs.
Time Freedom	You need to work according to your own schedule.

My Five Most Important Values

1.

2.

3.

4.

5.

Education and training

An essential part of knowing yourself and what you have to offer a potential employer or client is understanding the education and training you have received in your life. Many people tend to be very narrow when they address this issue and focus almost exclusively on the formal education that they have received. Your formal education is important but so is what you have learned informally from volunteer organizations, travel, research, reading, sports activities, artistic pursuits, hobbies, your religion, your culture, the Internet, social groups you belong to, and anything else you can think of that has influenced you.

Make a list of all of the formal education you have received and include any degrees, diplomas, and certificates you have earned. Also include a list of all of the informal education you have received and the things that you learned, any awards or trophies that you received and any commendations or praise you received for what you did.

From all of this, make a list of the subjects, courses, seminars, etc. that you liked the most and what it was about them that you liked. Identify areas you would like to include in your career.

Again, from all of your education and training, identify the subjects and areas that you disliked the most and what it was about them you didn't like. If you could chart your career from now on, which of these subjects or areas would you like to exclude from the work that you will be involved with?

From all of the above, what achievements are you most proud of and what is it about them that gives you the greatest degree of satisfaction or makes you feel good? Be sure to include all of your lifetime learning experiences, not just the ones from your formal education. Finally, rank these things in terms of their importance to you.

Weaknesses

The final component you need to be aware of to understand yourself is to recognize your weaknesses. Everyone has them. What areas do you need to work on and improve on? What skills need to be developed or updated and what new areas or technologies do you need to get some exposure to?

Appraising your career

Now that you have a clear picture of yourself from a personal point of view, you need to create a similar picture in terms of your career up to this point. From the following list (and again, feel free to add to it), select what you consider to be your top five strengths in terms of your career characteristics. Then come up with at least two examples of situations where you have shown these strengths. Finally, rank them in terms of their importance to you.

Career Characteristics

Able to Concentrate	Resourceful	Stable
Able to Handle Stress	Risk-Taking	Conscientious
Rational	Self-Controlled	Teachable
Analytical	Methodical	Creative
Persevering	Motivated	Businesslike
Efficient	Open-Minded	Logical
Versatile	Organized	Clear-Thinking
Enthusiastic	Thorough	Meticulous
Quick	Trusting	Supportive
Imaginative	Practical	Tactful
Independent	Empathetic	Tenacious
Attentive to Detail	Punctual	Diplomatic
Self-Confident	Accurate	Trustworthy
Mature	Reliable	Precise
Competent	Intelligent	Inventive

Career Characteristics — My Top Five Strengths

1.

2.

3.

4.

5.

```
Situations Where I've Shown Them

1.

2.

3.

4.

5.
```

Skills

Over your career you have accumulated considerable skills, and it is very important that you can readily identify these when you are talking to an employer or potential client. Often the decision to hire you is based on your skill set first and your personal characteristics second. Compile a list of your skills and group them into the following three categories: specialized, communication, and general.

Specialized skills are things like computer programming, designing graphics, compiling financial statements, and so on. Communication skills would include writing, teaching, motivating, directing, and mediating. General skills would include organizing, scheduling, compiling, initiating, and similar things.

Once you have compiled your list, select from it five skills that you most want to use in your career and give at least two examples of situations where you have applied these skills and what the outcome was in each case.

	Skills	
Specialized	Communication	General
1.		
2.		
3.		
4.		
5.		

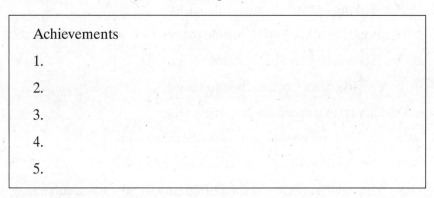

Situations Where I've Applied My Skills

1.

2.

3.

4.

5.

Achievements

Identify your successes and achievements during your career. Study your successes. Make sure you understand how you achieved the success and look for ways to apply what you did to your career from now on. What did you do? What did you learn? What did you enjoy? What did you accomplish? What were you commended for? List as many of these as you can think of and then select the top five in terms of their importance to you and your career. Finally, rank them in terms of which ones you are most proud of.

Achievements

1.

2.

3.

4.

5.

Interests

We have all developed preferences for the type of work that we do and activities that go along with that work, be it a job or a contract. From the following list, select the top three areas of work that you would most prefer to be involved with and in each case identify what it is about that area that appeals to you.

From the same list, select the top three areas that you would like to avoid if you had a choice and again, identify what it is about the area that you dislike.

Types of work

- Influence the attitudes or ideas of others.
- Gather information through direct contact with people.
- Help people with personal problems.
- Instruct other people in various tasks or skills.
- Supervise and be responsible for the work of others.
- Consult or advise others.
- Confront others, present them with difficult decisions.
- Investigate people by obtaining information about them.
- Provide service to others.
- Sell or market products or services to individuals or companies.
- Mediate between contending parties.
- Organize others, bring people together in co-operative efforts.
- Make decisions about others.
- Provide career counselling to others.
- Entertain or perform for enjoyment.
- Understand people and study their behavior.
- Develop and discuss ideas and theories.
- Make decisions based on definite rules and measurements.
- Explain or interpret ideas and concepts.
- Use materials or equipment in work, e.g., computers, graphic materials.
- Work with survey data or other information on public opinion.
- Conduct investigations or research.
- Work with documents and records.

My Three Favorite Areas of Work and What I Like
About Them

1.

2.

3.

Three Areas of Work I'd Like to Avoid and What I Dislike
About Them

1.

2.

3.

Your career/life highlights and lowlights

Everybody experiences ups and downs in their careers and in their
personal lives. As part of the process of defining who you are, what is
important to you, and what you want from your career, it is essential
that you be aware of these ups and downs and that you learn from them.

When analyzing your past, don't just focus on your work experience. Also include what you experienced outside of work when getting your education, participating in volunteer organizations, playing
sports, learning arts, and belonging to other groups.

Identify your favorite job or project and what it was about it that
you liked the most. Do the same for the companies/employers or
organizations, managers, and co-workers that you have worked with,
and again, include your experience outside of work.

Personal life

- What was the best decision you ever made in your personal life?

- What did you learn from it?

- What was the worst decision you ever made in your personal life?

- What did you learn from it?

School/college/university

- What were your favorite subjects in school?

- What was it about them that you liked so much?

- What subjects did you dislike the most?

- What was it about them that you disliked so much?

- Name some of the highlights of your school experience.

- Name some of the lowlights of your school experience.

- What achievement or achievements from your school years are you most proud of?

- What do your answers to all the questions related to your years in school tell you about the type of work you should be doing?

- What were your favorite subjects at college or university?

- What was it about them that you liked so much?

- What subjects did you dislike the most?

- What was it about them that you disliked so much?

- What projects or assignments you worked on in college or university gave you the most satisfaction?

- What was it about them that made you feel this way?

- Name some of the highlights of your college/university - experience.

- Name some of the lowlights of your college/university experience.

- What achievement or achievements from your college/ university years are you most proud of?

- What do your answers to all the questions related to your years in college or university tell you about the type of work you should be doing?

Career

- What was the best decision you ever made in your career?
- What did you learn from it?
- What was the worst decision you ever made in your career?
- What did you learn from it?
- What was your favorite job or project?
- What was it about it that you liked so much?
- What was your favorite company, employer, or organization?
- What did you like most about it?
- Who was your favorite manager?
- What did you like most about them?
- Who were your favorite co-workers?
- What did you like most about them?
- What was your least favorite job or project?
- What was it about it that you disliked so much?
- What was your least favorite company, employer, or organization?
- What was it about it that you disliked?
- Who was your least favorite manager?
- What was it about that person that you disliked?
- Who were your least favorite co-workers?
- What was it about them that you disliked?

Summarizing your career

From all of the preceding exercises, it is time to draw up a composite picture of yourself on the following chart. Include under each category the most important areas or things that you identified from the exercises.

Personal Characteristics	Values	Career Characteristices

Skills	Achievements	Interests

My Most Marketable Skills

1.

2.

3.

4.

5.

6.

7.

8.

9.

10.

"Know thyself" is an old but relevant saying, and now that you have taken the time to go through all of this analysis, you should have a pretty clear picture of yourself and what is important to you. It is critical that you have this before you get in front of a prospective employer or client, so take some time to reflect on this and internalize it.

At the same time, give yourself a pat on the back because you've done something that most people don't do. Like the athlete who trained hard and the actor who rehearsed well, you're now ready to sell yourself, and you'll do a much better job of it than your competition who, unlike you, haven't done their homework.

The final step in this process is to clearly identify what your most marketable skills are and where you want to apply them. From all of the above information, identify and rank what you consider to be your top five to ten marketable skills and again, get them clearly etched in your mind so that you can rattle them off any time you need to.

Let's also make sure that you know where you're headed in your career and why you're going in that direction by being very clear on what you want to do, where you want to do it and who you want to do it with.

The Type of Work I Want to Do

The Key Attributes of This Work

The Types of Companies or Employers I Want to Work With

The Key Attributes of These Companies or Employers

The Type of People I Want to Work With

The Key Attributes of These People

Succeeding as a Contractor

The workplace continues to go through the transition from being primarily job-centered, as it has been for over 150 years, to a more fluid mix of jobs and people turning to self-employment, including contracting. People who choose contracting, both those with considerable experience in the workplace and those just starting out in it, face numerous challenges, many of which will be new experiences for them. Following are some of those challenges and some things for the new contractor to consider.

Market yourself continually

There's a whole section on marketing yourself later in the book, but let's recognize the need for it at this point. Now that you've gone through an extensive analysis of your background and have identified your marketable skills and where you want to apply them, you're in good shape to tackle this challenge. You've also eliminated one of the biggest weaknesses people have when they approach this area, i.e., they don't take the time to go through the analysis that you just did and consequently they are not ready to sell themselves.

Even people who come from a selling or marketing background in the corporate world are challenged by this area. Selling yourself is a whole different scenario from selling products or services for a company, and these people, like most others, commonly do a poor job of defining their marketable skills.

You know more about selling than you think you do. When you were a kid, you did a pretty good job of it when you wanted something from your parents. As a parent, you're constantly doing it (or trying to), in steering your kids in the direction that you would like them to take.

So drop the notion that you don't know anything about selling; it's not true. Besides, you have no choice if you want to be successful. Even with your selling skills, you have the same challenge the sales professionals have: the need to continually sharpen those skills and to monitor which techniques are working for you and which ones aren't working.

Success for large companies comes in part from knowing that they must continually find new and better ways to sell their products and services. So must you. You'll always be challenged to know more about yourself, your skills, and why people would buy them. Knowing yourself and your market, both current and prospective, will be a daily challenge from now on.

Build up your network of contacts and potential clients. Sharpen your selling skills and be alert to the changes that are always taking place in the market. Finding time to sell yourself and line up new contracts when you're currently working on a contract is a challenge that any experienced contractor will readily attest to, but it's something that you must do.

You simply have to internalize the fact that your livelihood depends on how well you know your market and sell your services, so give it the priority it deserves. Finally, don't be modest or reticent. Be proud of your successes and the set of skills that you've developed, and recognize that you will be helping your client or employer by getting them to use those skills. This is one of the keys to confidently selling yourself.

Broaden your vision

People who are new to contracting have a tendency to think too narrowly in terms of what their skills are and the potential market for them. For example, if you speak more than one language, that could be an asset but only if you see it as one and are always alert to situations in the market where you could use it. If you understand cultures and systems outside of the country that you live in, that could be a marketable asset too.

If you have spent most of your career in one industry, that experience can be applied in other industries too, but many people often fail to see this. If you are a qualified accountant, it doesn't follow that your services are limited to situations directly related to the financial services area. Your education, training, life, and work experiences give you a much broader repertoire of skills that you have to offer.

An example of how people who are looking for work are making their challenge more difficult for themselves was given in an NBC News television feature in June 2008 that looked at people in the US who were struggling to find work and the financial challenges they were facing. They interviewed a man who had lost his job as a designer with one of the three big US automobile manufacturers in Detroit. He had been looking for a job for months and things were so bad he was getting up at 2:00 a.m. to deliver newspapers, this being the only work he could find. His wife said "If he doesn't find work soon as an automobile designer, we're sunk." It was obvious he and his wife saw their only option was to replace his job as an automobile designer with a similar job in that industry. Poor choice. Things are so bad in the US automobile sector he needed to look for work elsewhere. He was defining himself too narrowly as an automobile designer. He was a designer, period, with skills that could be applied in different industries. If he saw himself that way and was willing to accept contract, temporary, or part-time work, particularly with small companies, his chances of finding work would increase significantly.

If you're like most people, one of the things you learned in analyzing your career and life skills in the previous section is that you have interests and skills that you've never used. You may also have detected areas of work that you're attracted to and suited to that you've never seriously considered as areas where you could earn a living. Now's your chance to get rid of any type of narrow thinking. One of the positive aspects of the transition that the workplace is going through is that people are finding ways to earn a living in areas that they find much more interesting and fulfilling than those that they previously worked in.

Hone your communication skills

Your ability to communicate effectively becomes far more significant when you are self-employed versus when you are in the corporate world. Everyday skills such as communicating via a computer to being able to quickly get someone's attention about what you do and its value need to be sharp and continually polished. Having marketable skills means nothing unless you convince someone that they will benefit from using them, in terms that make economic sense for both of you.

All of your marketing materials, from your business cards to your résumé or brochure, your website and anything else that you use should project a professional and consistent message about your services and the benefits of using them. You also need to be ready at any time to verbalize this message in a succinct, persuasive manner.

Among the various skills that you need to be a successful contractor, good communication skills are imperative. If they are not a high priority with you, they need to be. Professional communicators such as actors, news broadcasters, and commentators are continually practising and honing their skills. If they have to do that to stay on top and be successful, so do you.

Commit to continuous learning

One of your ongoing challenges is to always be learning about yourself and your skills, the markets that you sell to and those that you would like to sell to, why your peer contractors are successful, why you get the business you get, why you're not getting the business you'd like to get, and the issues and trends going on in the market that affect you.

Consider the following questions:

- Are you stretching yourself in a positive way?

- What have you learned in the past six months?

- What would you like to learn in the next six months?

- Are you on top of the trends in your field?

- Do you know what skills you need to sharpen or pick up to ensure your future success?

- Do you review the projects that you have completed to see what you learned from them?

- Do you schedule training and education during times that you know will be slow?

- Do you regularly study the latest literature in your field?

Don't confine your learning to what is being offered by the traditional educational outlets or the profession that you belong to. Leading-edge trends and information are available via the Internet, some television programs, and other media as well as meetings and seminars that are held in your community.

Recognize that among the many hats you wear, training manager should be one of them. Training for you, that is.

Stay on top of the market

In days past, the workplace was a much simpler place and it was easier to stay in touch with what was going on. To stay informed today, you need to be much more vigilant and creative. As we have already noted, large companies are no longer the centres of activity. Most of the action these days is found in small companies. Since they don't have public relations or communications departments feeding the media about their activities, you need to develop a keen sense of smell to sniff out what is going on.

We have also noted that most of the work opportunities these days are hidden, so if you're not aggressively monitoring what is going on in the market, you're going to miss out on a lot of these opportunities. The Internet is a useful tool for staying connected these days, but how effective it will be for you is directly related to how creative you are in using it. Casual or occasional surfing on the Internet will not suffice. You need to develop a strategy for monitoring the websites that are important to you and invest some time to find out what these sites are. The websites you monitor will depend on what type of work you do and what kinds of work you are looking for.

When news comes out on trends and important events in the workplace, what is your typical reaction to it? Did you anticipate these things or did you already know about them? You need to be much more informed about what is going on in the workplace than the average person is if you want to succeed in today's work environment. That means knowing which types of media are useful to you, be it print, television, the Internet, or newsletters you subscribe to, and just being alert to things going on in your community.

Talk to successful contractors and you will find that they are always very well informed about what is going on and are seldom surprised by events when they are reported in the mainstream media. That is due in part to them having an effective network of contacts. How you can develop a similar network is covered later in the book.

Market research is one of those areas, like getting regular exercise and eating sensibly and so on, that everybody agrees is important. Talk to those who are struggling in today's workplace and you will consistently see that they approach market research passively or simply don't understand how important it is.

Go where the action is

If you're connected, you know where the action is. Get focused on those areas; find out who the players are and what companies are the leaders. When making the transition into contracting, there is a temptation to market yourself into the areas that you are familiar with. If the growth in these areas is flat or declining, stay away from them.

Use your own judgement and observations about what is going on in the market. Question what is being reported, don't take it as gospel. Not all of the "hot" areas of growth that we hear about in the media are necessarily so. Don't assume that the people doing the reporting are experts in these areas. Feel free to question what they are saying and compare it to what you are learning about what is going on in the market. Scrutinize statistics closely. Often what appears to be news is based on data that is several years old.

Don't eliminate specialized areas of growth as prospects because you have no experience in the area. There may be opportunities to sell your skills there. For example, not everyone who works in the IT sector is a technological wizard. These companies, like all other companies, need experienced accountants, administrators, materials managers, human resources personnel, and so on. If you do target this area, you better get informed about what is going on in it. Obtain a reasonable level of computer literacy and be ready, in broad terms, to talk their language. There's also a way to approach these companies that is covered later in the book.

Watch your finances

The financial implications of contracting are more complex than they were when your career was job-centered. Your cash flow will probably be erratic. Remember when you land a nice contract that it might be some time before your next one is in the hopper. Most people would benefit from advice from an accountant or financial manager who is experienced in dealing with self-employed people.

We tend to take things for granted when we know that a paycheck is being deposited into our bank account every two weeks. Now, you need to adjust your attitude about your finances. In between contracts, you'll still have expenses, so keep a close watch on them.

One of the questions that people who are new to contracting struggle with is how much to charge for their services. In broad terms, you need to know what the going rate is for your type of services, but it's far from being that simple. Large, successful companies periodically resort to sales or other promotions to increase business in slow times. If things are slow for you, you may have to be more flexible in your pricing than you would be otherwise.

How much you charge is often a function of how badly you want the business, how busy you are, and other factors. Don't give your business away, but don't be too inflexible in your pricing either. You'll find yourself thinking on your feet on this one more than you'd like.

Finally, talk to an accountant to get on top of all of the tax implications of your business and the records that you have to keep. Use quiet times to keep this area up to date; don't leave it all until the end of the year.

Avoid stock options

A prospective client may offer you stock options in lieu of cash payments for your services. This is quite common these days in the IT sector, especially with new companies. Forget it. Notwithstanding the fact that a few individuals have done well from picking up stock options that they later cashed in when the company became successful, it's not usually a viable option.

Leave the stock options to the venture capitalists and other professionals who know what they're doing and who are willing to take the gamble. Tell prospective clients that you operate on a fee-for-service basis only, i.e., you get paid in cash for the services that you provide.

Manage your time effectively

Eliminating tire-kickers quickly is a skill that you need to develop. When people respond to your marketing efforts, especially when you are new to contracting, you tend to be flattered and excited and you don't pay as much attention to qualifying them as you should. They may need your skills but can't afford them. They may be stingy or have cash flow problems. You could invest a lot of your time before you find out about these problems.

Know what your terms are — how much you charge and when you expect to be paid — and get them on the table as fast as you can. Serious prospects will not be offended by this. Be very alert at this time also to their body language and any other signs when you are talking about payment terms. If your gut tells you that there might be a problem with a potential client, your gut is probably right. Never enter into a contract if you have any doubts about the client's ability or willingness to pay you.

If the assignment is a long one or needs a lot of preparation on your part before it can begin, come to an equitable financial arrangement with the client to ensure that some cash is flowing your way. If you become concerned about a client's ability to pay you after you've started a contract, cover yourself. Don't hand over any reports or other information that they want until they pay you. If you do hand over the results of your work without being paid, you've lost control. Forget about suing them; the only ones who win in lawsuits are lawyers.

The new self-employed contractor often has a tendency to be shy about getting to the specifics about when and how much they will be paid. Eliminate that type of thinking or it will cost you dearly. The only people who will be offended by approaching your payment terms in a businesslike manner are those you want to stay away from in the first place.

Saying no to potential business is sometimes the smart thing to do. Know your limitations both in terms of what you can deliver and how much time you can commit to a project. Refresh yourself on weekends and make time for personal priorities like family, exercise and self-improvement. You're not Superman, so don't try to be. You're not perfect and you'll make your share of mistakes, especially when you're new to contracting, so don't beat yourself up when you do.

Your body will signal you when you need to back off, slow down, or laugh at yourself or the world. Listen to these signals and act accordingly. Remember, nobody ever went to their grave saying "I wish I had spent more time at the office."

Increase your physical/mental fitness

One thing you would be wise to do in making the transition to contracting is to make a commitment to yourself to increase the level of your physical and mental fitness. Being a contractor is more demanding than being employed in a full-time job. You will have your share of disappointments and times when you wonder if you're going to make it.

The way you'll get through these times and minimize their effect on you is to toughen up your mind and your body. You don't have to become a marathon runner, but you better get out in the fresh air on a regular basis and do something physical. There are opportunities to do this without making major disruptions in your life. Walk or cycle instead of driving whenever possible. Walk up stairs instead of taking the elevator. Get up half an hour earlier and do some stretching or get in a quick run or walk.

Make your diet healthier by reducing your intake of alcohol, fatty foods, and desserts. If you smoke, try to quit or at least cut down. Your doctor will be happy to help you do this.

Your mind is like your stomach; you can fill it with junk and pay the price or enrich it and reap the benefits. Monitor what you read and what television programs you watch. The library is full of biographies of people who started out with nothing, faced incredible hardships in their lives, yet went on to great success. Seek these out and read them. You can't help but be inspired by their example.

Spirituality has become a common term in our vernacular. It can refer to anything from traditional religion to modern techniques for meditating. Spirituality has been an integral part of every group and race of people in the history of humankind and it is a part of your background, regardless of what ethnic group you belong to. From this you can conclude that spirituality is important, and if it is not a part of your life, you're missing out on something relevant.

Spirituality in the workplace is a topic that is gaining popularity among employers. In the past three years, at least a dozen large conferences on spirituality in Canadian workplaces have been held. While the benefits of spirituality are hard to measure statistically, feedback from employees in companies that encourage and facilitate it shows increases in employee motivation, creativity, and job satisfaction as well as better relations with colleagues and supervisors.

Practical benefits of exercise

The personal benefits of incorporating regular physical and mental exercise into your lifestyle should be obvious, but there are practical business reasons as well, and companies are realizing the payoff in encouraging their employees to live healthy lifestyles.

"Quiet Rooms" are increasingly showing up in the offices of the more progressive, informed companies: Places where their employees can retreat to practise yoga, do Tai Chi, or to pray or meditate, the benefit being an increase in staff satisfaction and engagement at work.

According to Jennifer Crispen, a professor at Sweet Briar College in Virginia who teaches a course in the history and culture of women's sport, two-thirds of female business executives and 75 percent of all chief executives exercise regularly, saying that this cultivates business essentials such as self-discipline, goal setting, and self-confidence.

Exercise in the morning notably improves your workplace performance that same day, according to research from Leeds Metropolitan University. Hiring managers like to see candidates with athletic experience, since sports can teach workplace values such as teamwork, shared commitment, decision-making under pressure, mental toughness, and focus.

Compensation packages that include health club benefits are more and more common, as are health care packages that cover non-traditional medicine, these being of particular interest to young workers.

Stay flexible

One of the most common mistakes made by people who are new to contracting is not being flexible enough when determining what they will do or what types of assignments they will accept. There's nothing wrong with looking at something that would be considered a lateral move or a move up from the job that you had; just don't make it the only thing that you will consider.

Don't equate taking on a contract with being hired for a full-time job. If the assignment you're taking on isn't at the level that you're used to, so what? It's only a contract, it's not permanent. The important thing is that you're back in the game, making money, expanding your network, and who knows where it could lead? One thing you can be sure of is that by landing a contract position, you increase your chances of finding something better in the future versus staying unemployed and holding out for a better position.

Eliminate any thought that you may have that there's any stigma attached to accepting a contract at a level below where you were in the past. It's quite the opposite. Your friends, promoters, and colleagues will admire you for finding work and besides, nobody needs to know exactly what you're doing. If anyone asks, tell them the truth, you're working on a contract at so-and-so company, period.

Take a broader perspective. While the current workplace is no picnic for a lot of people, things will improve at some point. When they do, there will be opportunities for those people who were smart enough and gutsy enough to stick it out in the tough times, found work, expanded their network, and maintained a positive attitude. Make a commitment now that you're going to be one of those who will capitalize on the opportunities that will come along when the market picks up.

You're a capable, experienced individual with more to offer the world than you give yourself credit for. Look at all avenues, give your imagination a boost. Do not restrict your options to things directly related to what you have done in the past. There's a whole world of alternatives out there.

There are people who have lost their jobs and who have found a way to make a living doing something that previously was only a hobby and completely unrelated to their career. There are lots of others who are unemployed and vegetating who would consider such an idea goofy and off-the-wall. Find what it is you love to do and just do it.

CHECKLIST 1: PREPARATION

☐ Do you have a clear understanding in your mind about what you want to do, what you have to sell, and how it will benefit those who buy it? Could you verbalize these things quickly and in a proactive way if you ran into an old acquaintance or got a telephone inquiry?

☐ Are you excited about what you're doing or are about to do? Have you moved beyond your dependency on a job? Do you recognize that many people are making a living as contractors and that you will do that too?

☐ Do you look and sound like a contractor? Are you ready to sell yourself at any time?

☐ If an opportunity comes up for you to do some business, are you clear on what your terms will be? How much will you charge? What will your payment terms be? Are you ready to eliminate tire-kickers?

☐ Have you increased your connectivity to what is going on in the workplace? Are you constantly alert to all of the relevant media coverage on workplace issues?

☐ Do you have a financial plan in place for your business? Do you have a system in place to keep track of all your expenses? Do you know what your accountant will ask you for at the end of the year and do you keep right on top of this area?

☐ Have you committed to increasing your physical and mental fitness? Have you blocked out times for these activities on your schedule? What specifically are you going to do to increase your effectiveness over the next three months?

SELF-COUNSEL PRESS — HOW TO FIND WORK IN THE 21ST CENTURY 09

3
HOW TO MARKET YOURSELF

Bite off more than you can chew — then chew on it.

— *Mary Kay Ash*

Sales and Marketing Defined

These two terms are used interchangeably and sometimes create confusion because in traditional terms, they mean quite different things. First of all, marketing is something that precedes selling. It refers to a wide range of activities that have as their objective getting the attention of potential buyers of a product or service.

These activities can be anything from a sophisticated, expensive television commercial or infomercial to someone walking around a busy shopping area with a sandwich board strapped to them that is promoting a product or service. Selling is what happens when you get the attention of a prospective buyer and they call you, walk into your store, or visit your website.

Myths About Selling

The idea of having to sell oneself is something that makes people uncomfortable for a variety of reasons. They don't understand what is involved. They incorrectly assume that they won't be any good at it. They perceive, again incorrectly, that because they're not salespeople, they can't do it. Finally, they have a completely false notion about what successful salespeople do.

The myth of the back slapping, loud, aggressive, sales type is just that, a myth. When was the last time you bought something from someone like that? Successful salespeople are professionals who are well trained, attend to the needs of their customers, and are genuinely interested in helping them. They sell solutions to problems and products and services that satisfy a genuine need. Some of the most successful salespeople are quiet, unassuming people — not quite the stereotype often attached to salespeople. The main reason why they're successful is that they're sincere. Their customers pick up on that because sincerity can't be faked.

The average person may be nervous about selling oneself but shouldn't be for any of the preceding reasons. Nervousness arises because of unpreparedness. If you did a good job of defining exactly what you have to offer a potential customer or client, as explained in Chapter 2, you are ready. That's why so much emphasis was put on that whole process. You've done what the vast majority of people never do, i.e., take the time to identify their marketable skills. No wonder they're nervous. Intuitively, they know they're on shaky ground before they start.

Good salespeople are not born that way. They've been educated and trained by professionals and have lots of experience, and you can be sure that they've fallen flat on their face in front of a customer or client on more than one occasion. Good salespeople have some characteristics in common with good athletes. They've developed the skills to be successful but if they ever get complacent or lazy about keeping those skills sharp, they're in danger of getting their butt kicked.

They're also resilient. Every successful salesperson endures a lot of rejection before they get to a successful sale. Anyone who is easily discouraged and who can't regularly bounce back from disappointments will have a difficult time in sales.

Your selling challenge is to communicate to a potential employer or client how they can benefit from using the skills that you have already identified. Not in a fancy, forced, or insincere way but in the way of having a normal conversation with someone.

What makes you different?

You already know the answer to that question. You know what your top five personal and career strengths are, your skills, values, the successes you've had, and how companies and people have benefited from those successes. Before you meet with a potential employer or client, you need to give some thought to how your skills and successes can help them. So let's look at how you do that.

Preparing for an interview or meeting

Before you get in front of an employer or client, you've got some homework to do. You're half-ready at this point in that you know what your skills, strengths, and successes are. Now you need to fill in the other side of the equation. How are those going to help this employer or client? You need to find out as much about them as you can by doing the following:

1. Study (not just look at) their website, annual reports, and any other material you can find on the company. If you show up for a meeting and ask questions that could easily have been answered by studying their website, you're in trouble. You don't deserve to get their business because you haven't prepared yourself for the meeting in a professional way.

2. Look at their competitors' websites. You'll get a broader view of their industry this way and you may even get some ideas that they haven't thought of yet. You may also be able to access industry or association websites for the particular sector that they are in and find out what the current issues and hot topics are for that sector.

3. Go to the library and get all the latest trade journals, magazines, professional association newsletters, and magazines that relate to the industry the company is in and look for recent developments and trends. "Google" both the company and the industry to see what information that might bring up.

4. Focus on the key issue that will determine whether or not you get hired or get their business, i.e., how can my skills, experience,

and successes help this company? Another way to look at that is to ask yourself, what value can I add to their operation?

5. As you gather all this information, keep in the back of your mind the question "Would I fit in well with this company or industry?" You spent a lot of time in Chapter 2 defining what was important and relevant to you in your career, what your values were, and so on. Is what you're finding out about this company and industry compatible with your values and interests?

If it is, that will increase your enthusiasm for joining them. That enthusiasm will come across in an interview, where of course you will share this fit with the company representative.

Ideally it would help to talk to an employee of the company to hear how their experience stacks up against the information you've come up with. Since that's not always possible, another way to get some insight from an insider may be to solicit feedback from people who know the company on a blog that you subscribe to or on a blog related to the company's industry.

The way professional salespeople are trained in this area is to get the customer focused on the features and benefits of their product or service. Here's a feature of my product or service and here's how it can benefit you. You do the same thing. Here are my features and here's how they can help you.

A few final points: Talking too much is the most common interview mistake job candidates make, according to a May 2006 survey by executive search firm Korn/Ferry International.

According to a February 2006 survey by Robert Half International, 86 percent of Canadian executives said that employment seekers should follow up within a week of submitting an application, something that they often don't do or are reluctant to do. Follow-up is essential, so much so that if you aren't going to do it, you needn't bother to apply.

You've done everything right and one of the companies you targeted has responded to your marketing efforts and has asked you to come in for an interview. The interview is going really well when they suddenly ask you "Why should we hire you?" How should you respond to this?

First of all, assume ahead of time that they will ask you this, so you won't be caught flat-footed. Second, they wouldn't be asking you this if they weren't interested in hiring you. A professional salesperson would correctly see this as a buy signal.

Finally, don't try to answer the question with some grand or profound response. They liked the points you made in the marketing material you sent to them; that's what got you the interview. So simply go over those again. And then stop talking.

Now you have a complete arsenal for success. You know what your key strengths are and you know how they can help the company. So what do you have to be nervous about? Nothing. Get in there and get the business.

The marketing metaphor

Before you market, you must:

- be clear on the qualities of your product and how it benefits the buyer.
- identify the market you want to go after.
- determine what marketing tools work best for you.
- continually hone your selling and marketing skills.

Ask any experienced contractor what their biggest challenge is and the odds are they will say marketing and selling their services. There is no one, proven way to do it. You have to use a variety of approaches and monitor the results to see what works and what doesn't work. Let's look at some of the marketing tools that you can use.

Marketing Tools

Advertising

One of the most challenging issues that contractors have to deal with is advertising. It's also a challenge for large companies. Success in advertising is elusive and it's a moving target. Even if something works once, there's no guarantee that it will work the next time you try it. There's no one way to do it. Some successful contractors never advertise in the conventional sense, but you can bet that they are always very alert to any opportunity to market themselves. You can also bet that they have an effective network and are well informed about what is going on in their field and in the industries that they want to penetrate.

Other contractors, who have impressive résumés, brochures, websites, and other marketing materials, and who regularly spend money on advertising, may be struggling. One of the most frustrating things about advertising is that there is no guarantee when you spend your money on it that it will work. You only find out after you have tried it. If you run an ad in a trade journal, for example, and you don't get a single call from it, you can't ask for your money back; it doesn't work that way.

Nevertheless, you have to do it. The big question is, how? You may feel you have a great deal to offer to your clients, but that means nothing unless you can get their attention and convince them to buy your services. Most of us learn how to do this by trial and error, and the commercial graveyard is full of great ideas and products that never made it.

So, somehow you have to advertise your services to the world. How you do it, what will work, and what is affordable given your limited funds to spend on it are all issues you will have to address. Fortunately, there are some guidelines to follow that will increase your chances of success.

Design an advertising plan

Before you grapple with all of the options that are available to you, there are some basics that you need to be very clear on.

Who are your potential customers?

How well do you know the market you are targeting? Who typically would make the decision to buy your services or hire you? What print material do they read? What associations do they belong to? What trade shows are they likely to attend? What are their purchasing criteria and options? If you were in their shoes, what is it that you're offering them that will get their attention? What problem do they have that you are going to solve? As one wag put it, "Look for their pain."

If you are sending marketing material to them via regular mail or email, make sure that it is addressed to the individual that you are targeting and not to some generic title like "President." It will take time to find out who your contacts should be but it's time well spent versus taking the generic approach, which rarely works.

What value are you offering?

How are you going to solve their problem and how does that compare to the options that they can get elsewhere? The key here is to be sure that your skill set is a good match for the types of challenges your customers are likely to face in their industry, and since you've done your homework you will be comfortable knowing that you're targeting people who are a potentially good match.

What is so unique or special about your offer that will get their attention? Are the benefits of your service clearly spelled out or are they implied in broad generalizations?

How much will you charge?

You can be sure that your fee will be a factor in the decision to purchase or not. How will the potential client know that they're getting good value for what they're buying? Remember that value is not all about pricing; if it were, the only stores that would be around would be discount stores.

Your marketing material must emphasize that your pricing is competitive, that you have proven skills that they can access, that you are genuinely interested in helping them, and that you will back up any claims that you're making about what you will deliver.

Spread out your funds

Don't blow all of your advertising budget on one event. Be selective and design an advertising plan with several options. As you try each one, monitor the results and learn from the experience. Always track where your success is coming from. Ask people who call you how they heard about you and modify your plan to focus on the areas that work. Don't panic when things don't work out as well as you'd like them to. Large companies with years of experience in advertising go through that too.

Build customer loyalty

Once you have a client, make sure that they're happy with your service. Even if the contract is for a short period of time and not worth a lot of money to you, treat the client the same way you would if it were a long-term, lucrative contract. You never know where any given contract is going to lead. A satisfied client is your most powerful marketing tool if you know how to use it and you use it wisely.

A good time to ask a client if they know of any other companies that could also benefit from your services is when you get positive feedback from them. People who are new to contracting are sometimes reluctant or shy about asking for referrals. There's no need to feel that way. If you approach them in a polite, businesslike way, they will be happy to refer you to other potential clients.

There are many sophisticated advertising and marketing techniques available, but nothing works better than word of mouth. If you have happy clients, you can bet that the word will get around; even so, don't forget to give them a gentle nudge just to be sure that it does.

Finally, there's a fundamental fact that if you are new and even if you are prepared to spend significant funds on advertising, success comes slowly. It takes time to get established and to build credibility in the marketplace. That's easy to say but not so easy to swallow when you're investing your time and money trying to get yourself established and things aren't moving as fast as you would like them to.

There's an old maxim that comes from the I Ching: "Grow slow and send your roots deep." That's good advice to follow.

Get publicity

As a self-employed contractor, you may not see any connection between publicity and your work. You may be surprised at the opportunities that exist for you to get some publicity. It's not just world leaders, sports stars, and celebrities that the media report on; they also write about ordinary people and events going on in the community.

Most newspapers have a regular section on new businesses that are starting up in their area, and they often provide a free service to announce start-ups. Check out both the main and community newspapers in your area to see if they have such a service and if they do, be sure to get yourself included in it when you start up.

If you belong to an association, they often make similar announcements about their members in their monthly newsletter, so again, make sure that you get your service noticed when you start up. This might prompt a call from people that you haven't heard from in a long time.

While getting publicity is new territory for contractors and learning how to use it is a challenge, it can be a fun thing to do. It's your chance to let your hair down and show how creative you can be. Here are some ideas to get you going.

Professional and community associations

If you belong to groups like this and you're not on the executive committee, find a way to get on it. If you don't belong to any groups, you should look around to see what's out there and join any that you can make a contribution to and at the same time, spread the word about your services. This is a win-win situation for you and the group that you join. You're making a genuine contribution to their cause and increasing your profile at the same time. You will find that successful contractors use this strategy effectively to market their services.

If there's something unique about what you do, that could be newsworthy if you contact the right people, reporters, or publishers. If you have solved a problem for a client that was significant and it has application to other companies, don't keep that information to yourself; get the word out there.

Participating in trade shows and events in your community can be an inexpensive and effective way of marketing your services. You don't have to have a large display at a major trade show to do this. Look for community events, chambers of commerce, and other professional/business groups who are putting on events that might offer a good chance for you to advertise and do some networking.

You might want to make something happen in your community by spearheading a fund-raising event. Be the primary participant in it or align yourself with a professional/ business or volunteer organization to achieve something along these lines. How about organizing a raffle to raise funds for a worthy cause? Or donating a prize or an award to some deserving individual or group in your community?

If what you do is connected to a national trend or an area of community interest, how about writing an article about it and sending it to your local newspaper or other media outlet?

If you are knowledgeable in an area that the public knows little about or could benefit from, share that knowledge with your community.

You may also want to impart this knowledge by offering yourself as a speaker at a monthly meeting of a business or volunteer group in your community. These groups are always looking for speakers of interest.

Maybe there's an opportunity for you to start up a new group in your community with you as the first president. How about an association of self-employed contractors that provides a forum for these people to share their experiences with their peers?

Get others to promote your business

Large companies spend a lot of time and resources on database marketing and other sophisticated marketing techniques to get the maximum return from one of their most valuable assets, their existing customers. On a smaller and simpler scale you can do that too.

We've already touched on the importance of getting referrals from your customers. They can help you in other ways too, and most of them will as long as you approach them in a discreet way and pick the right time to do it. Just don't be pushy or insensitive about this area or it will backfire on you. Here are some ways that a happy customer can help you.

Even better than a simple referral where the customer gives you the name of one of their contacts is for them to introduce you to the contact. That sets a very positive tone for you to do business.

Perhaps your customer belongs to a group or an association that you would like to belong to but can't get into without a sponsor or an invitation to join from an existing member. The first step would be to join your customer as their guest at their monthly meeting.

If they really appreciate your services, they may even be willing to promote you in some way. You could get a notice in their company newsletter or the newsletter of a professional association that they belong to. They may be willing to provide a link from their website to your website.

If you have brochures or other promotional material about your services, they may agree to display this information in a conspicuous area on their premises. You may simply give them some extra business cards of yours to pass around.

No matter what type of help you get from a customer, make a point of thanking them and maybe offer a simple gift or other token of your appreciation. Also make sure that they know that you will promote their business any time you find an opportunity to do so. Ask them for some of their business cards and marketing materials.

Social marketing

If the service you offer could benefit a volunteer or charitable group that you admire and respect, consider offering your services to them for free or at a generous discount from what you normally charge. You have to be sincere and sensitive in your approach to them and not come across as self-promoting or trying to capitalize on their visibility in the community.

Handled properly, this can be an effective way for you to raise your profile in your community. There are probably groups that you share common beliefs and values with that would be grateful to receive some type of non-monetary assistance.

Look around and you will see lots of examples of these types of strategic, win-win relationships between volunteer and charitable groups and large and small businesses, as well as prominent people in the community who lend their names to help organizations promote their services and raise funds. There is probably an opportunity for you to do that too.

Direct marketing

Direct marketing is a legitimate way to market products and services by mass-mailing promotional material, and some companies do nothing else but direct marketing on behalf of clients. It's not a good way for you to go though. Your approach should always be a targeted one and not a shotgun approach, which direct marketing often is. It makes sense for some companies to get into mass-mailing, but it doesn't make sense for you.

The only exception to this will be if the service you offer has great potential for a particular sector of industry and there are a lot of companies in that sector in your area. Even so, you still want to make sure that your material is going to a specific individual and is not addressed to a title in a company. You should also test that sector with a small sample and see what type of results you get before committing to a larger mailing.

Blogs

Blogs are one of the fastest growing areas of the Internet, and some people are finding them an effective way to market themselves. But beware, this is not an area for amateurs, for people who approach this tool superficially, or for those who expect instant results.

A well-executed blog can set you apart as an expert in your field. A poorly executed blog will make you look like a lightweight and a novice in your field. To create an effective blog requires a significant amount of your time, particularly in the beginning, but once you have created it, you will also need to commit a lot of time to keep it relevant and interesting.

Blogs are in some respects akin to newsletters. Many so-called newsletters are no more than a rehash of news items that their authors have gleaned from the Internet and other sources, and readers are quick to pick up on this and dismiss them.

If you are an expert in your field and are prepared to invest the time it takes to create and maintain an effective blog, it can be an effective marketing tool and be good for your career. Some describe it as the new public relations tool and, assuming it is well executed, it could be more effective than a website. Here's what a blog can do for you:

- *Attract recruiters, hiring managers, and employers* who scan the Internet looking for specialists in various fields. But that's a double-edged sword. You need to be sure nothing you've said in your blog will turn these people off.

- *Raise the profile of your website.* Google indexes and rates websites in a way that makes blogs come up highest in Google searches.

- *Give you a creative way to network.* The time you invest to create and maintain an effective blog can pay off by portraying you as an expert in your field and letting you connect with the players in it. It also gives you an opportunity to make a positive contribution to your community.

- *Keep you on your toes* and on top of what is going on in your field. Those who realize they are putting themselves "out there" in view of their community will make sure that what they have to say is topical and relevant.

- *Help you launch a business.* If your product or service is unique, a blog could be a way to quickly and effectively connect with the market you're targeting, versus the more traditional means of advertising.

While blogs continue to grow, most people still don't use them. According to a May 2008 study by Forrester Research, only a quarter of the US adult online population reads a blog once a month. Among Internet users, 14 percent of men and 11 percent of women blog according to the Pew Internet and American Life Project.

Multiply yourself

One of the more common mistakes made by people who are new to contracting is putting all of their employment options into one basket. This leads to erratic cash flow, and the ups and downs of operating this way are hard to deal with psychologically. You need to generate as many potential revenue streams as you can.

Most people, if they put their minds to it, can find more than one way to sell and apply their skill set. Successful contractors always have several sources of revenue, and they are always cultivating them and looking for new areas where they can apply their skill set.

The payback from the various options is not always equal. It's more common to have a range of potential revenue, depending on where and how you are selling your skill set. That's not a bad thing. It's better to be busy and making some money than to be idle, waiting for a lucrative contract.

Not all activities can be evaluated strictly on the amount of money that you get directly from that source. For example, teaching part-time at a college or university or in the private sector can be a very effective way for you to raise your profile in the community and market your services. You won't get rich on what you earn from teaching, but it can be a good way to network and pick up some business.

If you have a skill set that is unique or that can help people or businesses, consider putting together a seminar. You can do this on your own or in conjunction with a college, university, or a professional association. The financial return will be higher than teaching a regular course at a college or university, and you will have a better chance of picking up some business from those who attend.

Accounting, engineering, and other professional services companies may be good areas for you to target. A lot of their work is project oriented, and they often find themselves short-staffed and in need of temporary help.

If you belong to a professional organization, take advantage of the employment services that most of them offer to their members. Get to know the people who run it and keep in regular contact with them.

Your communications network

Your communications network is a fancy way of describing the methods you provide to the world to contact you and the impression that they get when they do try to contact you. Some people unwittingly make it hard for potential clients to reach them or they are sloppy about the way they respond to inquiries. Here are some suggestions for you to consider:

- If someone is trying to contact you, you need to know right away so you can get back to them quickly. Cell phones, pagers, and Personal Digital Assistants (PDAs) such as BlackBerrys are most commonly used for this. If you don't respond quickly to inquiries, you may find that the prospect has found someone else by the time you do get back to them. You will be putting a lot of effort into trying to get prospects to call you. Don't blow your chances of getting their business by not responding to them as quickly as you can.

- In today's fast-paced, 24/7 world, employment seekers who have PDAs could have an advantage over those who don't. Recruiters are increasingly using them as a primary communications tool. They allow both the recruiter and the employment seeker to communicate regardless of where they are, versus relying on voice mail or picking up emails from their PC. PDAs give both parties a virtual home office. Communicating effectively via a PDA takes some thought and experience. You need to keep your message brief in consideration of the small screen. You need to get to the point quickly and focus on the key items you feel will be of interest to the recipient. To get the recipient's attention, you may need to be more creative with your subject line than you would be with conventional emails. You probably need to develop a more informal writing style. And finally, given the immediacy of communicating with these devices, there's a temptation to send responses in a hurry. You still need to communicate in a thoughtful, effective way and take time to proofread your message before you send it.

- If you work from home and your telephone line is the primary means of contact, be aware if you are tying up the line by being on the Internet or making a lot of calls. A prospect should never get a busy signal if they are calling you. At the very least, they should get a businesslike response that says you're temporarily tied up but you will get back to them shortly. If they do get a busy signal, or if you don't get back to them right away, you may well lose their business.

- Fax machines are intended to be available at any time, unattended. Make sure that yours is.

- Watch how you respond to calls, especially if you operate from your home. Always assume that the call is a business call and respond appropriately.

- Be very alert to the names of the people you're sending your marketing materials to and the names of their companies. If one of these people responds to your marketing efforts and you answer in a way that clearly shows you don't recognize them and/or their company, you will make a very poor impression and probably eliminate yourself as a candidate.

- Check your email regularly and respond to inquiries immediately.

All of the communications tools that you need to look like a professional are readily available today from telecommunications providers. It is imperative that you know what these tools are and what they can do for you and that you avail yourself of them to project a consistent, professional image.

QUIZ 2: YOU, THE BRAND

1. What are your most marketable skills?

2. What skills would make you more employable if you acquired them?

3. What courses, seminars, trade shows, or other events are coming up in the next few months that will give you an opportunity to upgrade your skills?

4. Identify some accomplishments in your life or career that would appeal to a potential employer.

5. What do these accomplishments say about you?

6. Identify some accomplishments or activities from your college/university years that would appeal to a potential employer.

7. What do these accomplishments or activities say about you?

8. Name some people you admire and would like to emulate. Identify some of the characteristics they have that you would like to have.

9. What type of company would you like to work for? Name some of the attributes or values it would have that would attract you to it.

10. Name some companies that have the values and attributes you just identified.

11. Blogging is a great way to market yourself. True or false?

12. Write a job description for the type of job you would love to have.

SELF-COUNSEL PRESS — HOW TO FIND WORK IN THE 21ST CENTURY 09

Résumés and Marketing Materials

Cover letters

Never, ever send out a résumé without a well thought out and complementary cover letter to go with it. The format is one page and a short one page at that. It must be very marketing oriented. Its objective is to get the recipient interested enough in you to go on and read your résumé.

To do that it must clearly address the needs of the individual and company you are sending it to and further indicate that you can help them with those needs. It should quickly establish the fact that you know something about the company and their industry. A generic, vague cover letter will invariably go straight to the garbage along with the résumé.

Here are some things to consider:

- If you have any doubts whatsoever about the spelling of the individual's or company's name that you are sending your résumé to, make sure that you get both of them right before you send it off.

- Does the letter convey a clear message that you can help this company and contribute to their bottom line?

- Make sure the letter conveys the fact that you know something about the company and the industry that they're in.

- Make sure that the content is positive and upbeat.

- Make sure that the letter complements what you are saying in your résumé.

The cover letter in Sample 1 is designed to go with the twenty-first century résumé that is illustrated later.

Marketing letters

A good marketing letter can be an effective way of getting a decision maker's attention or arousing their curiosity. All decision makers/ business owners are interested in increasing sales, decreasing expenses, and making their operations more efficient, so focus on those areas.

Sample 1
COVER LETTER

1695 Edgewater Street

North Vancouver, BC V7N 4M8

Phone: (604) 555-8881, Fax: (604) 555-9999, Email: jaf@direct.ca

Date: _____

Dear _____

In my career as an Information Technology manager, I sometimes found myself short of experienced people when trying to meet the requirements of the various projects I was managing at any given time. My budget did not give me the option to hire experienced contractors through large consulting companies.

I'm aware that you have several large projects coming up and if they present a staffing problem for you, I may be able to help you. As an independent contractor, my rates are affordable and I can offer you a diverse set of current IT skills on a part-time or full-time basis. As you will see in the attached résumé, I have extensive experience working with non-IT personnel from senior managers to clerical staff. I relate well to their needs and challenges in working with MIS systems.

I work equally well in a team environment or on my own and I have extensive project management experience. If you could use a hands-on IT professional who will produce results right from the beginning, I would like to hear from you.

I will follow up with you by telephone within a week. If you would like to contact me in the meantime, please call me at (604) 555-8881 or email me at jaf@direct.ca.

Sincerely,

Joe Flynn

SELF-COUNSEL PRESS — HOW TO FIND WORK IN THE 21ST CENTURY 09

You may have some expertise or experience operating in an area that they couldn't otherwise afford to hire on a permanent basis. You may also be valuable in a strategic role working with the president or business owner or as a mentor to some of their younger, inexperienced staff.

As part of your requirement to be connected to what is going on in industry, be on the lookout for news about companies who are expanding, restructuring or who you deem may benefit from your expertise. Find out who the decision maker is and send them a marketing letter. Follow these guidelines:

- Keep it to one page.

- Get directly to your expertise and how it may benefit them.

- Omit any small talk.

- Focus on their needs, not yours.

- Show them that you know something about them.

- If you have accomplished something in your career that you think would be of interest to them and would have some application in their operation, highlight it.

- Your age is not important. Keep the focus on what you have accomplished in your career.

- Don't specify your rates but emphasize that they are affordable and cost-effective.

- Emphasize how flexible you are in terms of working part-time, full-time or on any terms that suit their needs.

- Emphasize that you are a pragmatic, roll-up-your-sleeves type who will work with them to implement whatever changes are required versus a consultant who writes reports about what should be done.

- Offer to meet with them, with no strings attached, to explore how your skill set may be of benefit to them.

- Say you will follow up within a week and do so.

Spend some time on marketing letters. They can open up doors for you and are worth the investment of your time to get proficient at them in. See Sample 2.

Sample 2
MARKETING LETTER

1695 Edgewater Street
North Vancouver, BC V7N 4M8
Phone: (604) 555-8881, Fax: (604) 555-9999, Email: jaf@direct.ca
Date: _____

Dear _____

In my career as an Information Technology manager, I sometimes found myself short of experienced people when trying to meet the requirements of the various projects I was managing at any given time. My budget did not give me the option to hire experienced people from large consulting companies.

I'm aware that you have several large projects coming up and if staffing them is a problem for you, I may be able to help you. As an independent contractor, I can offer you very attractive rates and I will work with you in any time frame that makes sense for you.

I can offer you a diverse set of current IT skills with application in a wide area. I'm equally comfortable working on my own or in a team and I have an extensive background in project management, including experience in your industry.

I can operate at the detailed, technical level and can also contribute to the development of strategic plans to enhance the effectiveness of MIS systems. I relate well to both IT and non-IT staff, from clerical staff to senior managers.

I noticed on your website that you have undertaken a program to upgrade the IT skills of your staff throughout the organization. I successfully designed and implemented a similar program for one of my clients and upgraded the IT skills of 250 of their staff members. If appropriate, I would be happy to work with you on that program.

I will follow up with you by telephone within a week. If you would like to contact me in the meantime, please do so at (604) 555-8881 or by email at jaf@direct.ca.

Sincerely,

Joe Flynn

SELF-COUNSEL PRESS — HOW TO FIND WORK IN THE 21ST CENTURY 09

Résumés

There is a wide range of opinions on the effectiveness of a résumé as a marketing tool when looking for work and even more opinions on what it should look like. You can purchase any number of books today on how to create an effective résumé, while some commentators suggest that you throw away your résumé and get out and bang on doors and network like crazy.

There is no one, simple tool to describe yourself or one, simple way to look for work. You should have a number of tools and use them interchangeably depending on what your objective is at any given time. A historical, chronological résumé may be appropriate if you are applying for a job where the skills required are a close match to what you have to offer. It is not an effective tool if you are targeting prospective companies looking for contract work.

Many people make the mistake of trying to come up with one, perfect résumé. Since your résumé should be targeted to the needs of the company that you are contacting, it should highlight the strengths that you have that match that company's needs. You need to select from the skill set you have to offer and the skills that are appropriate for that company and design your résumé accordingly.

That doesn't mean a complete rewrite of your résumé for every company that you apply to, it just means making some modifications to it to emphasize your most marketable skills that will appeal to them. The standard software that comes with today's PC allows you to make these modifications fairly easily.

In today's workplace, decision makers are more interested in the skills you have to offer and can apply as soon as you walk in the door than broad generalizations about what you have done in the past. Just like a good brochure or marketing document, the résumé you are preparing at any given time should anticipate the needs of the company you are targeting and focus on how your skills and experience can help them.

Today's résumé must be much more marketing oriented than résumés of the past. Its primary function is to generate enough interest in you and what you can do for the company you're contacting that they will pick up the telephone and call you.

Many current résumés are attuned to yesterday's workplace and are therefore ineffective. What can you do for me today? That's what decision makers want to know. Not what your title was in your last job or what you've been doing for the past twenty years. The emphasis must be on who you are and what you can do for that company.

The layout and presentation must be professional looking. Use white, letter-quality paper only, no colored paper or expensive paper that would be more appropriate for a wedding invitation. Any spelling errors or typos will probably guarantee that the résumé will go directly into the garbage.

Use a laser printer and make sure that the layout, spacing, use of different fonts, etc. give the résumé a professional look. Your aim is to produce a businesslike document that shows that you took some care in creating it. That won't guarantee you anything, of course; it's just the minimum standard you have to meet.

If you send out a résumé that looks like a copy of a copy that was run off on a corner grocery store's photocopier, with the printing not properly lined up and maybe some toner marks on it, there's a good chance it will go directly into the garbage. Why would anyone want to hire someone who was that careless about the way they were presenting themselves? The tool that you use should reflect how you see yourself and what you have to offer.

You should also be able to respond immediately if you get a response to your résumé. If you suddenly get a telephone call about a résumé that you sent out some time ago, will you be ready to respond in a way that confidently backs up what it says or would you be caught unprepared and mumble some weak response?

The product you are selling is you, and it is imperative that you take time to internalize your vision of yourself and to make sure it is consistent with the picture you are painting with your résumé and other materials you use to market yourself.

The following examples show different ways to portray the same individual.

Comments on the traditional résumé in Sample 3

This is typical of a résumé that would have been acceptable in yesterday's workplace. The layout, spacing, and use of fonts make it easy

TRADITIONAL RÉSUMÉ EXAMPLE 1

Joseph A. Flynn
1695 Edgewater Street
North Vancouver, BC
V7N 4M8

Telephone: (604) 555-8881
Fax: (604) 555-9999
Email: jaf@direct.ca

Education

Master of Science, Applied Mathematics, UBC

Bachelor of Science, Applied Mathematics, SFU

Many IT courses from IBM, Microsoft, and other major IT vendors

Career History

Urban Enterprises, Victoria, BC, 1995–2000

Director, Technical Services

Responsible for a team of 15 IT professionals in a centralized IT department with an annual budget of $2 million. Successfully met all user departments' needs for information retrieval from a corporate database and supported their staff in all IT functions.

Mercantile Fund, Vancouver, BC, 1990–1995

Manager, Information Services

Provided support and leadership to 250 IT users throughout the organization while managing 12 IT professionals.

High-Tech Consulting, Vancouver, BC, 1983–1990

Systems Analyst

After starting as a junior programmer, I worked my way up to a Systems Analyst position, where I worked on projects to meet the overall IT needs of the organization.

BC Lumber, Vancouver, BC, 1980–1983

Documentation Analyst

Responsible for the compilation and recording of various corporate reports.

Hobbies: Fishing, golfing, and gardening

References will be supplied on request

to read. If it was being submitted in response to an advertisement for a full-time job and if the applicant's experience were a close match for the position being advertised, it might get a positive response.

The individual's experience is presented in a very general way and there is no indication of what their achievements have been and how those helped the companies they worked for. Hobbies should be left out as should the line stating "References will be supplied" since it is redundant.

This résumé is inappropriate if it were being used to find contract work in today's market. It is not marketing oriented at all and gives no indication of the individual's strengths.

Comments on the traditional résumé in Sample 4

Sample 4 is an improvement over the previous example as it is more marketing oriented. Right at the beginning we get a snapshot of who the individual is, their experience, and an indication of the skill set that they have to offer.

This is followed by the most important part of the résumé, i.e., what the individual has accomplished in their career and how they helped the companies and people that they have worked with. This is the section that you would modify. Select and highlight the strengths that would be of most interest to the company that you are targeting at any given time.

Achievements are followed by a brief but adequate description of the person's work experience. You can elaborate on this all you want when you get in front of the decision maker. You may want to have a more detailed version of your work history available in case they would like to see that.

Educational qualifications are at the end and that's where they should be shown.

The Twenty-First Century Résumé
The Format
1. Your Name

2. Your Profile

TRADITIONAL RÉSUMÉ EXAMPLE 2

Page 1

Joseph A. Flynn

1695 Edgewater Street	Telephone: (604) 555-8881
North Vancouver, BC	Fax: (604) 555-9999
V7N 4M8	Email: jaf@direct.ca

A highly competent Information Technology executive with over 15 years' experience in different industries. Expertise in corporate systems planning, project management, and network and operating system architecture. Skilled in working with and in training non-IT managers and their staff.

Accomplishments

Managed and contributed to the development of a LAN network to meet the strategic needs of a marketing organization.

Managed the conversion of a custom software information system to a UNIX system for a financial company while meeting their ongoing daily IT needs.

Trained and managed 250 IT users during a major conversion of an outdated MIS system.

Achieved a 25 percent savings in IT costs by streamlining inefficient methodologies used by IT and user staff.

Worked with a group of senior managers to redefine the MIS system to produce more timely and relevant reports for managers and user personnel.

Planned, implemented, and documented systems and procedures for a disaster recovery plan to ensure the stability of an MIS system.

Developed, implemented, and taught an information systems management course for non-IT users to increase their awareness of and comfort level with MIS systems.

Sample 4 — Continued

Career History

Urban Enterprises, Victoria, BC, 1995–2000

Director, Technical Services

Responsible for a team of 15 IT professionals in a centralized department with an annual budget of $2 million. Successfully met all user departments' needs for information retrieval from a corporate database and supported and trained their staff in all IT functions.

Mercantile Fund, Vancouver, BC, 1990–1995

Manager, Information Services

Provided support and leadership to 250 IT users throughout the organization while managing 12 IT professionals.

High-Tech Consulting, Vancouver, BC, 1983–1990

Systems Analyst

After starting as a junior programmer, I worked my way up to the Systems Analyst position, where I worked on projects to meet the overall IT needs of the organization.

BC Lumber, Vancouver, BC, 1980–1983

Documentation Analyst

Responsible for the compilation and recording of various corporate reports.

Education

Master of Science, Applied Mathematics, UBC

Bachelor of Science, Applied Mathematics, SFU

Many IT courses from IBM, Microsoft, and other major IT vendors

3. Your Accomplishments

4. Your Career History

5. Your Education

6. Your Address and Contact Information

Your résumé should consist of one page only. Everything of importance that you need to say can easily be accommodated on one page. Don't forget, you can elaborate all you want when the company you're targeting calls you and sets up a meeting.

Remember also that you're not applying for a job here. You're marketing yourself and trying to get the employer's attention. So your résumé should zero in on your experience and accomplishments that your research tells you will be of interest to them. If you haven't done that research, you have no business contacting them and you're wasting your time doing so.

At the beginning of the résumé, show your name only.

1. In your profile, give a succinct, proactive description of who you are, your experience, and an indication of your skill set. Sample profiles are given later in this book.

2. From the accomplishments in your career, select and highlight those which will be of most interest to the company that you are sending your résumé to. Emphasize how your accomplishments helped the companies and people you have worked with.

3. In your career history, show the companies that you worked for, your title and the years you were there. Also include their website address. This makes it easy for anyone who is not familiar with the company to get a quick overview.

4. Show your education, including degrees, diplomas, etc.

5. Show your address and your contact information.

See Sample 5 for an example.

Sample profiles

A communications professional experienced in advertising, marketing and corporate communications. Strong computer skills include

Sample 5
TWENTY-FIRST CENTURY RÉSUMÉ

Joseph A. Flynn

A highly competent Information Technology executive with over 15 years' experience in different industries. Expertise in corporate systems planning, project management, and network and operating system architecture. Skilled in working with and in training non-IT managers and their staff.

Accomplishments

Trained and managed 250 IT users during a major conversion of an outdated MIS system.

Achieved a 25 percent savings in IT costs by streamlining inefficient methodologies used by IT and user staff.

Worked with a group of senior managers to redefine the MIS system to produce more timely and relevant reports for managers and user personnel.

Planned, implemented, and documented systems and procedures for a disaster recovery plan to ensure the stability of an MIS system.

Developed and taught a course for IT professionals to help them better understand the needs and challenges of non-IT users of MIS systems.

Worked with a group of marketing professionals to develop a corporate website to facilitate inquiries from customers about the company's products and services.

Career History

Urban Enterprises, Victoria, BC, 1995–2000   www.uei.com
Director, Technical Services

Mercantile Fund, Vancouver, BC, 1990–1995   www.mfc.ca
Manager, Information Services

High-Tech Consulting, Vancouver, BC, 1983–1990   www.htc.com
Systems Analyst

BC Lumber, Vancouver, BC, 1980–1983   www.bcl.ca
Documentation Analyst

Education

Master of Science, Applied Mathematics, UBC

Bachelor of Science, Applied Mathematics, SFU

Many IT courses from IBM, Microsoft, and other major IT vendors

1695 Edgewater Street, North Vancouver, BC V7N 4M8

Phone: (604) 555-8881, Fax: (604) 555-9999, Email: jaf@direct.ca

SELF-COUNSEL PRESS — HOW TO FIND WORK IN THE 21ST CENTURY 09

expertise in most current business software on both Mac and Windows platforms.

A high-energy senior contracts and purchasing professional with skills in customer service, problem solving, negotiation, computer applications, and the ability to build positive relationships with internal customers, contractors, and vendors.

A practical, hands-on, and action-oriented individual who enjoys working in a dynamic technical environment. A mechanical engineer and MBA graduate with demonstrated leadership, strategic planning, and decision-making skills and a reputation for coaching and developing people while delivering profitable results.

A marketing and communications professional experienced in the consumer and business product and service environments with a proven record of satisfying business objectives in the most cost efficient and effective manner.

A highly competent Information Technology executive with 24 years' experience including corporate systems planning, technical and development project management, and network and operating system architecture. Skilled in delivering enterprise systems solutions while building and motivating teams with diverse technical expertise.

An action-oriented financial executive who thrives on developing and executing corporate finance strategies to maximize shareholder value. Adept at developing effective organizations, championing change and motivating strong employee performance.

A financial management graduate with a keen interest and experience in Internet commerce. Speaks the language of today's IT personnel but relates primarily to the needs of the customers who use IT systems.

A fine arts graduate with excellent communication skills who is equally comfortable working on assignments independently or as part of a team. Current computer skills complement an interest and track record in the creative application of computer technology to achieve business objectives in the design of websites and other marketing materials.

A health sciences graduate with a background and keen interest in the application of non-traditional medical healing practices. Interested in working with organizations that apply a holistic approach to patient care.

A psychology/political science graduate, fluent in French, and well travelled. Interested in an overseas, project-oriented assignment with a multinational organization.

A mature MFA graduate with experience in graphic design. Interested in innovative design companies that work with architectural firms and the construction industry.

An MBA graduate with a background and interest in social entrepreneurship. Particularly interested in working with a non-profit organization that helps disadvantaged, poor, or abused women.

A civil engineer with a record of achieving results working with teams of technical and non-technical people on a wide range of construction-related projects. A hands-on achiever who needs little or no supervision. Comfortable in dealing with senior managers, tradespeople and other professionals. Experienced in current IT applications and project-management software.

Brochures

If you are going to operate as a contractor, a tool that you should seriously consider using is a brochure that describes you and the services you offer. Most people will benefit from the time and money spent on developing an effective brochure for the following reasons:

- By having a brochure, you immediately look like a contractor.

- The exercise of creating a brochure is beneficial to you psychologically in that it forces you to nail down exactly what you have to offer and the benefits. You will feel more confident about yourself as a result of the exercise and you will have brochures readily available to market yourself.

- You will make it easier for the promoters in your network or existing clients to help you to promote your business if they have some of your brochures to hand out to anyone in their network who they feel should know about you. Distribute them along with a cover letter to your network of contacts as soon as you create them.

Sample 6
BROCHURE

Side One

Joseph A. Flynn, M. Sc.

An experienced and accomplished Information Technology professional with an extensive background in project management who is ready to help you meet your short- and long-term IT needs.

Do you have an IT project that you need help with but can't hire anymore full-time staff?

Do you need an IT professional but can't afford to hire one from the large consulting companies?

Could some of your IT staff benefit from some training to improve their communication skills and working relationships with non-IT personnel?

Do you have an IT project that you have been putting off because you don't have an experienced manager to handle it?

Do you need help with some IT applications conversion or upgrading?

If you answered yes to any of these questions, I can help you to meet your needs at rates you can afford. I'm a hands-on achiever with a strong record in successful project management.

You can reach me at:

(604) 555-8881 or
jaf@direct.ca
Joseph A. Flynn, M.Sc.

Side Two

Sample Projects

Managed and contributed to the development of a LAN network to meet the strategic needs of a large marketing organization.

Trained and managed 250 IT users during a major conversion of an outdated MIS system.

Achieved a 25 percent savings in IT costs by streamlining inefficient systems and procedures used by IT and user staff.

Developed and taught a course for IT personnel to help them better understand the needs and challenges of non-IT users of MIS systems.

Worked with a group of marketing professionals to develop a corporate website to facilitate inquiries about the company's products and services.

Worked with a group of senior managers to redefine the MIS system to produce more timely and relevant reports for managers and user personnel.

Planned, implemented, and documented systems and procedures for a disaster recovery plan to ensure the stability of an MIS system.

I will be happy to meet with you, at no expense or obligation to you, to discuss how I may be able to help you with your IT needs.

(604) 555-8881 or
jaf@direct.ca
Joseph A. Flynn, M.Sc.

- Your brochure should look professional and must be specific about what you have to offer and how that benefits potential clients. You should be able to identify these things on both sides of a standard envelope-sized card stock that is available from printers or office supply stores. Do not spend a lot of money to produce a glossy, multicolored brochure that isn't necessary. The primary requirements are that it is simple, specific and that it looks professional.

- Your brochure is very similar to your marketing letter. You are stating the same information in a different format. Make sure that you emphasize your willingness to meet with clients, with no strings attached, to see if you can help them. Ask them to contact you by telephone or email to set up an appointment. Emphasize also that you are a hands-on professional who will work with them to implement whatever changes are required to improve their operation. Finally, always carry your brochures with you and be ready to distribute them along with your well-rehearsed description of what you are all about.

Sample 6 is an example that is intended to give you the gist of how to produce a brochure. In reality, it is what you would give to a printer or graphic designer, who could dress it up and create a professional-looking brochure.

Websites

The day is closer at hand than you think when companies who are hiring will ask applicants to electronically submit their URL (universal resource locator) or website address rather than a résumé. Eventually everyone will have a website.

We're not there yet, but given that websites are becoming easier and cheaper to produce, having one among the tools you use to market yourself is something you should seriously consider, especially if you have a lot of expertise to offer potential employers.

Simple and businesslike should be the primary considerations in creating a website, as you'll see in Sample 7. Like your brochure and other marketing tools, it must focus on the needs of potential clients and how they can benefit from the skill set you have to offer. Stay away from the "flash and splash" type of websites with heavy use of graphics, which won't impress anyone.

Joe Flynn   Information Technology Professional

| Home | Contacts | Portfolio | Links |

An experienced and accomplished Information Technology professional with an extensive background in project management who is ready to help you meet your short- and long-term IT needs.

Do you have an IT project that you need help with but can't hire any more full-time staff?

Do you need an IT professional but can't afford to hire one from the large consulting companies?

Could some of your IT staff benefit from some training to improve their communication skills and working relationships with non-IT personnel?

Do you have an IT project that you have been putting off because you don't have an experienced manager to handle it?

Do you need help with some IT applications conversion or upgrading?

If you answered yes to any of these questions, I can help you to meet your needs at rates you can afford. I'm a hands-on achiever with a strong record in successful project management.

1695 Edgewater Street   Email: jaf@direct.ca
North Vancouver, BC   Telephone: (604) 555-8881
V7N 4M8   Fax: (604) 555-9999

SELF-COUNSEL PRESS — HOW TO FIND WORK IN THE 21ST CENTURY 09

Having your website address on your business card makes you look more professional and makes it more powerful. If you meet someone at a networking event, for example, you can give them your business card and refer them to your website rather than giving them a brochure or résumé. You also make it easier for people in your network to get the word out about you to their contacts, since all they have to do is give them your business card.

A website may also get you noticed by recruiters, hiring managers, and employers who are increasingly scanning the Internet in their search for new staff. Following is a sample home page for the website of Joe Flynn.

Getting Organized

Given all of the alternatives that you have for marketing your services, a planned approach to what you want to achieve each week is advisable. The key items you must focus on are:

- Finding prospects. A prospect is a decision maker or business owner who knows what you do and has expressed enough interest to meet with you.

- Getting contracts. A contract is an agreement to pay for your services that accepts your financial terms, when you will be paid, what you will deliver, and when you will deliver it.

- Expanding your network, especially your promoters.

- Finding good target markets for future prospects.

Set weekly goals for each of these but be flexible, especially if you are new to contracting. Keep a record of what you are doing, what is working and what isn't.

Be careful not to let favorite or easy activities dominate your time. Sending out letters is easier than focusing on finding prospects by telephone or in person, but you know which one of these activities will determine your success or failure.

Monitor the progress of each of your prospects and always be clear on what the next step is to move it along to completion.

Continually pick the brains of successful contractors you know and follow their advice and examples for success.

Finally, stay flexible. While planning and organizing your time is very important, things rarely work out exactly as you think they will, and successful contractors will all tell you that everything takes longer than you thought it would. So stay loose and roll with the punches that you can be sure will come your way.

Sample 8 is a "Weekly Action Plan," a tool that you may find useful for monitoring and evaluating your marketing activities. You will also find one on the CD that accompanies this book.

Sample 8
WEEKLY ACTION PLAN

Weekly Action Plan for week							
Check When Done	Actions Planned	Phone Contacts Made	Brochures/Letters Sent	Marketing/Letters Sent	Additions to Your Network	Prospects	Contracts
	Monday						
	Tuesday						
	Wednesday						
	Thursday						
	Friday						
	Saturday						
	Sunday						

Networking Dos and Don'ts

There's probably no other word that is used more frequently in relation to today's workplace and that is more abused, misunderstood, and overused than "networking." That's unfortunate, because if you understand what networking is really all about and you're prepared to invest the time it takes to put an effective network together, it is probably the most powerful tool you can use to market yourself and find those hidden work opportunities that were discussed in Chapter 1.

Successful contractors always have an effective network and they are always cultivating and expanding it. But it took them years to put it together and that's the first lesson to learn. If you think that you're going to quickly create an effective network by attending as many meetings and so-called networking events as you can, you're kidding yourself; it doesn't work that way.

You need to develop a networking strategy that works for you and gradually build up your network. You've seen the people who race around trade shows, meetings, and other events frantically handing out their business cards and collecting as many as they can lay their hands on. So they end up with a fistful of business cards and think they've done a great job of networking. The question is, what are they going to do with all of those cards that they've collected? In reality, probably nothing. From a networking point of view, they're worthless.

If you attend a lot of networking events but don't have a good reason to be there, the odds are you won't connect with any people that you would want on your network but you may well get hustled by people who want to sell you something.

If you are selective about the events that you attend, and you need to be, networking will happen naturally. You shouldn't be there unless the event is about an area that you're interested in or would like to learn more about. Under those circumstances, you are more likely to meet people with similar interests and have a normal conversation with them. That's what networking is about.

So let's first make sure that you understand what effective networking is.

I'm uncomfortable doing it

If you're uncomfortable networking, you're not doing it right or your motives are wrong. If you only contact people when you need help, you're not a networker, you're a sponge. Remember our earlier discussion about selling yourself and why so many people are uncomfortable with it? Many of the same things apply here. If you're picking someone's brains for purely selfish reasons, you should be uncomfortable with that. On the other hand, if you are exchanging information with them, that's quite different.

If they are well informed about an area that you would like to know more about and you acknowledge their expertise and politely request their assistance and they agree to share some of their knowledge with you, there's no reason for you to be uncomfortable. You approached them openly and honestly and they responded positively.

It's okay to be a bit uncomfortable with networking until you really understand how it works, but have no delusions about its importance. There are no successful contractors who don't have an effective network, so it's a skill that you will have to develop.

It's ironic that some people who are shy about networking are always willing to help others who are seeking out their advice or trying to learn something about an area that they're very familiar with. When the situation is reversed, they suddenly become uneasy and feel that they are imposing on people.

Promoters and supporters

As you start to build up your network, approach people whom you know initially and build up your confidence gradually. "Promoters" and "supporters " are terms used to classify people in your network. Supporters are your family, friends, and people that you have worked with in the past. Promoters are people who you know are well connected to what is going on. Both types are important but the more promoters you get to know, the more successful you will be.

Most people are very sloppy about networking and that's one reason for their discomfort. Make it easy for people to help you. Take the time to explain to them what it is you're looking for. Make sure that they have copies of your brochure or your twenty-first-century résumé. That way if they think of someone they know who could help you, all they have to do is give them one of your brochures or pop your résumé in the fax machine.

The clearer the picture your contacts have about you and what you're looking for, the higher the probability that they will think of you if they run across someone who may benefit from using your skills.

Everybody has a network but when we attempt to document it, we have a tendency to be too narrow. Be as broad as you can when defining your network. Don't just include obvious choices like close business associates and friends. Include people from groups that you belong to now or have belonged to in the past. Alumni associations, professional and industry associations, former competitors, customers, co-workers, bosses, and people you have managed should be included. Sports clubs or community or volunteer associations that you belong to as well as cultural, arts, or religious groups are also helpful.

Network with a purpose in mind

Here are some ideas to keep in mind as you network:

- Try to expand your awareness of what is going on in the workplace. Be politely aggressive when soliciting information about things that are taking place. Who is expanding and hiring or who is leaving, possibly opening up an opportunity for you?

- Get the names of key contacts. As long as you are discreet and assure people that you will be professional and polite in approaching any people they know, they'll probably give you some names.

- If the timing seems right and you know the person well enough, ask them if they would mind introducing you to some of their key contacts.

- Ask for advice. If you're talking to someone who you know is well connected, ask them how they would go about networking if they were in your shoes.

- Always be ready to network. Never go anywhere without your brochures or marketing materials, and be ready to give a short, proactive description of what you are doing and what you are looking for.

- Finally, always make a point of thanking anyone who helps you and get into the habit of thinking, is there any way I can help the person who is helping me? As you get better at being connected to what is going on, be on the lookout for information that, while it may not help you, could be useful to someone in your network and be sure to pass it along. Good networkers are always sharing information with their contacts.

Networking tips and pointers

Definitions:

- Networking is really just talking to someone who can give you ideas, opinions, names, and advice. It is not selling but it is an opportunity to create a positive impression.

- Networking is a professional interaction, not a desperate plea for help.

- Don't worry about immediate results. People are very impatient when they are networking. If they don't walk away from a meeting or event with immediate results, they think they've failed. Just focus on building up your network and the results will come in good time.

- The trick is to build up your network when you don't need it. If you land a nice contract, don't get complacent about networking. Keep at it and expand it and nurture the contacts in your network.

- Don't abuse your network. Sometimes when business is slow there's a tendency to panic and get aggressive with your contacts. That will come back to haunt you. Keep your approach low-key and pace yourself and things will work out.

- Be prepared for networking. You spent a lot of time in Chapter 2 defining your strengths and marketable skills. One of the reasons for doing that was to prepare you for effective networking. Be ready at any time to give a short, proactive description of what you do and what you're looking for.

- There are actually people out there who enjoy helping other people, just for the sake of helping them. That's something to keep in mind if you're nervous about networking.

- People who have just landed a new job or lucrative contract could be good targets for you to network with. They must have been active networkers themselves and their contact information should be fresh. They can also empathize with your situation.

- Some people love to be asked for advice. It strokes their ego and makes them feel good.

- Be yourself. A common mistake made by people who are new to networking is that they think they have to become great communicators or salespeople. Just act naturally. If you are a low-key type, that's fine; good listeners make good networkers.

- Connect to your passion. Attend events that feature areas that are of interest to you and you won't have any problem talking to people.

Characteristics of successful networkers

- They live balanced lives. Unlike many others who are burning out in today's society, they are unlikely to make this mistake. To them, family, health, and personal and spiritual values are more important than business success. They know when to say no.

- They're well rounded, with interests outside of their work. They work to live, not live to work. Being informed is important to them, and they make a point of allocating time in their schedules for this, unlike others who always have a pile of magazines, journals, and other material that they plan to get to sometime.

- They invest time and money to continually hone and sharpen their skills. They will know about seminars, courses, trade shows, conferences, and other events that are coming up that will help them to add to their skills and which, coincidentally, are also good opportunities to network.

- They avoid typical networking events that are continually being promoted by amateurs and others with a vested interest in attracting uninformed but well-meaning employment seekers.

- They are very clear about what they have to offer, the companies and industries that would be interested in the skills they have to offer, and how their services will benefit potential clients. Being constantly alert to opportunities to expand their network and client base is a mind-set they've developed, not something they do between assignments.

- They contribute to their profession. You will find them serving on the executive and committees of the associations they belong to. They're genuinely interested in the advancement and promotion of these associations and generously share their expertise with the other members.

- They contribute to their communities. They're givers, not takers. They give generously of their time and expertise to at least one non-profit or charitable association, and you will find them serving on the boards of these groups.

These characteristics have been developed over time, and these successful networkers will readily admit that they've kissed their share of toads and wasted time at events that in hindsight they should have avoided.

QUIZ 3: NETWORKING

1. What activities are coming up in the next couple of months that might be good opportunities for you to do some networking?

2. If you attended a networking event full of the type of people you would like to connect with, what would they be talking about?

3. Outgoing, gregarious people make better networkers than quiet, reserved people. True or false?

4. Successful networkers are givers who consistently share their knowledge with no expectation of anything in return. True or false?

5. Name at least one non-profit or charitable organization that could benefit from your time and expertise if you were willing to give it.

6. What trade, professional, or other such organizations would it be beneficial for you to join?

7. The best time to network is when you're unemployed, about to graduate, or when your job or contract is about to expire. True or false?

8. The more networking events you attend, the higher the probability you'll find work. True or false?

9. Is there a need for a new association or special interest group in your chosen field? Are you willing to get it started? Are you willing to be the president or head of it?

10. People who are shy about networking or uncomfortable with it are often very helpful and accommodating to others who need help or information from them. True or false?

SELF-COUNSEL PRESS — HOW TO FIND WORK IN THE 21ST CENTURY 09

There's no such thing as a perfect networking strategy. People who are new to networking and who are uncomfortable with it need to be careful not to dismiss events in advance just because there's no guarantee they will yield results. They need to get themselves out there and be prepared to kiss their share of toads too.

Looking for Work on the Internet

In today's workplace, the Internet is an essential and invaluable source when looking for work opportunities and for keeping abreast of what is going on in the world. It is mandatory that you know how to do basic research on the Internet.

Email is no longer an option. It is every bit as important as the telephone and in some areas of business it is more important. Make sure that your email address is on every piece of marketing material you produce.

When approaching the Internet as a research tool, think of yourself as a prospector looking for gold dust. Sure a gold nugget now and then would be wonderful, but if you approach your search expecting to find nuggets, you'll be disappointed.

Just like the prospector, don't expect the gold dust to come easy either. You'll have to shovel your way through some data before you find what you're looking for, and you will have to use your creativity too.

Any research librarian will tell you that the good information is hidden and you have to be aggressive and diligent to find it. If you're not comfortable with doing basic research on the Internet, contact your local library. Many offer free courses to show you how to do it.

Be realistic in your expectations of finding work on the Internet. Richard Bolles, author of the perennial best-seller *What Color Is Your Parachute?*, suggests that the average person has only a 2 percent chance of finding work on the Internet. He suggests that figure can climb to 45 percent for people who qualify for computer-related jobs listed on the Internet. This may be true for those with leading-edge technology skills that are still in demand, but it's unlikely that the average worker in the computer industry is any better off than their counterparts outside of it.

Drake Beam Morin, a large international consulting company that specializes in outplacement services, regularly surveys its clients on this topic. According to their studies, close to 70 percent of their clients say they found work via networking, while only 6 percent say they found it on the Internet.

All of the big job sites have impressive numbers of listed jobs, and this can lead to complacency and unrealistic expectations on the part of employment seekers who register with them. What these sites don't usually tell you is the number of applications they receive for these jobs. Most observers who track these things suggest that only 3 to 5 percent of employment seekers find employment through online job sites and that at least 80 percent of the employment opportunities available at any time are not listed on these sites. So be realistic about your expectations if you register.

You might be better off registering with a local job site or one that specializes in your field. And this area is changing constantly, so you'll have to be diligent in monitoring these sites and be alert to new ones coming onstream that might be of interest to you. And finally, be careful about the personal information you post on the Internet, because identity thieves might be looking at it too.

What you need to monitor

The Internet is increasingly becoming the media of choice for companies looking to hire people and for people who are looking for work. There are thousands of job boards on the Internet at this point, and most company websites have a section where they list their current employment opportunities.

Obviously, as part of your objective to be connected to what is going on in the workplace, you have to be monitoring these websites. While there are thousands of sites to follow, in reality, there will not be many sites that are of interest and value to you. Unless you want to relocate, you're only interested in the work opportunities in your area, and that narrows your options considerably.

The main newspapers in your area will have their own job boards and you will want to monitor those as well. Some work opportunities will be listed on the websites of various associations in your area and since you know what companies you want to target, you will look at their sites too.

You still want to monitor the employment section of your newspaper, but you will see that more and more ads ask you to respond to them electronically and give you their email address or website address or both. Watch for more companies to give their website address only. In part, what they are saying to you is don't bother sending in your application until you have studied our website.

Companies will increasingly send you to their website and make you go through a series of screening steps, and only after you have successfully done that will you be given the chance to submit your résumé.

Electronic résumés

Electronic résumés are another marketing tool that you must have if you want to take advantage of the work opportunities that exist today. You should have several of these. One should be in plain text, with no special characters, bolding or underlining, since that's the format that many companies ask for. Another should be in word processing format and would look the same as the twenty-first century résumé, shown previously. You could use this one to solicit individuals whose email addresses you have and who you have found out from networking or research are good prospects for you to contact.

When you submit your résumé it will probably be scanned by software that is designed to screen out unwanted applications. It does this by looking for keywords in the résumé. For example, in the Information Technology area, résumés would be scanned looking for keywords that indicated that the applicant had experience with current software packages and areas like "project management." If you were applying and had experience in these areas, it would be imperative that you include these words or phrases in your résumé.

Sample 9 outlines a sample electronic résumé.

Note that in comparison to the sample twenty-first century résumé previously shown, this one contains no bolding or underlining. Note also in the Profile section that keywords have been added. These are the type of keywords that the screening software would be looking for.

Don't underestimate the significance of these keywords. Recruiters, hiring managers, and employers are increasingly running résumés through a keyword scanning process as the first step in screening

Sample 9
ELECTRONIC RÉSUMÉ

Joseph A. Flynn

A highly competent Information Technology executive with over 15 years' experience in different industries. Expertise in CORPORATE SYSTEMS PLANNING, PROJECT MANAGEMENT, and NETWORK and OPERATING SYSTEM ARCHITECTURE. Skilled in working with and in training non-IT managers and their staff. Experience with LAN, WAN, NOVELL, ORACLE, UNIX, SUN, and TELECOMMUNICATIONS.

Accomplishments

Trained and managed 250 IT users during a major conversion of an outdated MIS system.

Achieved a 25 percent savings in IT costs by streamlining inefficient methodologies used by IT and user staff.

Worked with a group of senior managers to redefine the MIS system to produce more timely and relevant reports for managers and user personnel.

Planned, implemented, and documented systems and procedures for a disaster recovery plan to ensure the stability of an MIS system.

Developed and taught a course for IT professionals to help them better understand the needs and challenges of non-IT users of MIS systems.

Worked with a group of marketing professionals to develop a corporate website to facilitate inquiries from customers about the company's products and services.

Career History

Urban Enterprises, Victoria, BC, 1995–2000   www.uei.com
Director, Technical Services

Mercantile Fund, Vancouver, BC, 1990–1995   www.mfc.ca
Manager, Information Services

High-Tech Consulting, Vancouver, BC, 1983–1990   www.htc.com
Systems Analyst

BC Lumber, Vancouver, BC, 1980–1983   www.bcl.ca
Documentation Analyst

Education

Master of Science, Applied Mathematics, UBC
Bachelor of Science, Applied Mathematics, SFU
Many IT courses from IBM, Microsoft, and other major IT vendors

1695 Edgewater Street, North Vancouver, BC V7N 4M8
Phone: (604) 555-8881, Fax: (604) 555-9999, Email: jaf@direct.ca

them. The sheer volume of résumés that some of them receive makes this a necessary step.

John Sullivan, a professor of management at San Francisco State University, tells of a study where researchers created 100 perfect résumés for an advertised position, ran them through an applicant tracking system that screened them for keywords and found that only 12 percent of them were picked as qualified. In other words, almost 90 percent of the résumés from qualified applicants were rejected because they were missing the right keywords.

So it's important that you know the types of keywords employers are likely to be looking for. The more you research the company and know about the type of work they do, the type of projects they work on, the type of people they already have and their backgrounds, the more likely you are to come up with the keywords the scanning process will be looking for. If you're responding to an advertisement in the newspaper or on the Internet, you should be able to glean some keywords from the way they've described the position and the qualifications they say they're looking for.

Note that you will have to tailor the keywords on your résumé to the company you're applying to at any given time, rather than having a set of generic keywords that you use for every company.

Online personas

When people create personal websites, participate in blogs or social networks like MySpace, FaceBook, or Bebo, write articles that are published online, or enter any other information related to them on the Internet, they're creating an online persona in the public domain for all to see.

According to a July 26, 2006, survey by Salary.com and AOL, the average worker in the US fritters away about two hours a day, mostly by surfing the Internet for personal use. Indiscriminate sending of emails has created a bonanza for some lawyers, as has been shown in such high-profile cases as Enron and other notorious corporate scandals. Even Microsoft chairman Bill Gates has had emails he has sent come back to haunt him in his legal battles with the US government. Employees have lost their jobs because of emails and blog postings sent via their companies' computers that are deemed to be offensive or in bad taste.

Having an online persona can be a double-edged sword. If you've been careful about what you've said, if you are alert to the potential consequences of the online persona you're creating and are always polishing and enhancing it, you could be creating a valuable asset. If you're careless or flippant about what you communicate on the Internet, you could be creating a liability. One recruiter suggested that you should manage your web presence or your online identity in exactly the same way as you manage your financial credit statements.

Increasingly, career counsellors at colleges and universities are getting feedback from recruiters and employers that information they've found on the Internet about students whom they've interviewed has eliminated them as serious candidates. What these students thought would be seen as funny, cool, or outrageous by their peers is seen in an entirely different light by recruiters and employers.

Similar stories are being heard from admissions officials at graduate and professional schools. Damaging information found online can raise serious questions about the student's maturity, judgement, values, and other personal attributes that are important to admissions officials. Students naively often have the view that the social networks or blogs they subscribe to are their (and their peers') domain and that the adult world doesn't know about them. The reality is that this information is in the public domain and accessible by anyone.

On the positive side, some recruiters and headhunters are finding that entering a few carefully chosen keywords on an Internet search engine can yield more prospects for positions they want to fill than can the more conventional ways of soliciting résumés. According to a 2005 survey of executive recruiters by ExecuNet, a Connecticut-based executive job-search and networking organization, 75 percent of recruiters were using search engines like Google and ZoomInfo to check out job candidates. One can expect that today that percentage is even higher. A survey of job seekers in early 2006 showed that 70 percent of them had been contacted "out of the blue" by someone who had found their contact information on the Internet.

Finding work via social media sites

FaceBook, MySpace, LinkedIn, Twitter, Flickr. These are just a few of the many social media sites available today. A March 10, 2008 "Shifting Careers" column in *The New York Times* under the heading of "The Web 2.0 résumé" asked for feedback on how effective these sites were as tools for finding work. Here are a few of the replies:

"The approach worked ... my current employer found me via my blog."

"As a 50-something, I do object to the repeated use of the word young. These tools are good for all employees — and in fact could add some buff to an older person seeking to underscore his or her 2.0 street cred."

"I believe many people need both the new media résumé and the old."

"I would really encourage people to have this sort of alternative format available and "linked" to on their traditional résumé."

"I think this is a fun, cute idea with very limited application ... the most important fact is does it sell you enough to get the interview?"

"Overall, this addendum to the traditional résumé format has been very well-received by potential employers I've interviewed with. Times are changing!"

"MANY, MANY, MANY companies refuse to allow their recruiters to use video/web résumés like this when assessing job candidates. The old-fashioned résumé is not going anywhere soon."

"I think anyone looking for a serious job in law or finance would be well advised to avoid this sort of nonsense."

"Most major companies block all social websites. This will not be a component of any HR recruitment plan."

These comments show the wide range of opinion on how effective social media sites are in finding work. Some people use them exclusively and are having success in finding work. Others avoid them like the plague. Some continue to use traditional résumés but give employers the option to find out more about them via the links they provide on their résumés to their social media sites. A survey of 100 Canadian senior executives conducted by Robert Half International showed that 26 percent would accept video résumés, according to an August 20, 2008 report in the *Globe and Mail*. Colleges and universities are increasingly using these sites as a way to recruit and interact with prospective students. Some companies are also using them as a way to evaluate how their customers and the public in general view them and the products and services they offer. Some professionals find Facebook to be a more effective and dynamic tool for keeping track of their contacts than the traditional Rolodex.

A June 2008 CBS NEWS television program looked at how some students are using tools beyond the traditional résumé to connect with employers at Career Fairs. It showed two students who were attempting to market themselves with YouTube videos. Their videos were very amateurish and predictably were getting them nowhere. A third student had created her résumé in the form of a ladies magazine that looked very professional. The company that hired her said that they were "blown away" by her approach.

Some students and experienced people naively think that just because they are using social media sites to market themselves, this will portray them as savvy and get the attention of employers. Not true. Obviously from the comments above, some companies won't even accept submissions in this format. And if this format is used, the same rules that make traditional résumés effective apply. They must be created in a professional, effective way that focuses on the needs of the employer you are targeting at any given time, assuming of course that your research has shown that they accept this format.

CHECKLIST 2: MARKETING

☐ How are you going to market your services tomorrow, next week, and next month? Do you have a marketing plan? Who are you going to sell your services to?

☐ What are you doing to expand your network of contacts, especially the promoters? When you find new people to include in your network, are you taking time to educate them about how they can help you?

☐ What if one of your promoters passes along your telephone number to one of their contacts? What impression will they get when they call? Will they hear someone who is upbeat, professional, ready to go? If you're not available when they call, how long will it take you to respond to their inquiry?

☐ What specifically are you doing to advertise your services? What plans do you have to improve your advertising over the next three months?

☐ What workshops, meetings, seminars, trade shows, etc., are happening in your area over the next couple of months? Which of them are you planning to attend? What is your networking plan when you do attend?

☐ Are there any charitable, church, business, sports, or community groups that could benefit from your services? Do you have a plan to contact them?

☐ When you send material to people about your services, are you specific about the action you want them to take? Will you specify that you will follow up with them?

☐ Have you taken advantage of the various free resources that are available in your area to promote your services?

☐ Are you on the executive committee of the groups that you belong to? Are you maximizing your opportunities to promote your services through business and professional associations?

☐ Do you have a list of websites that you monitor regularly? How many newsletters do you receive?

☐ How often do you check your email? Is your email address on every piece of information that relates to your business? When you correspond with people, do you make reference to your email address?

☐ Have you created at least one electronic resume?

☐ When you run across good, informative material on the Internet, are you sharing it with the contacts in your network?

☐ What are you learning from the Internet about other contractors?

☐ Are you finding that when news is reported in the mainstream media you are often already aware of it because of your connection to the various websites and newsletters you receive?

☐ What would a search on the Internet reveal about you?

SELF-COUNSEL PRESS — HOW TO FIND WORK IN THE 21ST CENTURY 09

4
GETTING STARTED

It's kind of fun to do the impossible.

— Walt Disney

Payback Time

Having made it this far in the book, you're now ready to reap the rewards for all your efforts. You can be excused, given the amount of work you've had to do, if you wondered at times if it was really necessary. The answer, unequivocally, is yes.

The payback for all your efforts is that you are now miles ahead of your competition. Sadly for them, the average person who is looking for work is doing a very poor job of it. They don't understand today's workplace and approach looking for work in much the same way their parents and grandparents did in the twentieth century.

They use one tool only, a traditional résumé or CV that is not tailored to the needs of the employers they're targeting. They don't like selling themselves, mostly because they don't understand what it is all about. And they don't prepare themselves adequately for interviews. Recruiters, hiring managers, and employers will all readily attest to the poor quality of the résumés or CVs they receive and how ill-prepared many applicants are for interviews.

You've eliminated all of these deficiencies and will stand out in a positive way with these recruiters, hiring managers, and employers. Regardless of how challenging the workplace may become due to outsourcing or economic conditions, you're on a solid foundation to succeed in the twenty-first century workplace. So approach your search for work in a confident, relaxed manner.

Pre-selling tasks

How easily can you answer the question "What do you do?" If the answer doesn't easily roll off your tongue, you've got some work to do. You have to be able to answer this at any time, particularly at networking events, in a positive, upbeat, confident, and persuasive manner. You need to be able to sell yourself at any time.

- If you've decided to earn your living as a contract worker or to start a small business, determine the name you're going to operate under. Give this careful thought; it could be costly if you decide to change it down the road. If you feel that you need a title, decide on that too. People who are new to this area tend to give more importance to titles than is justified. Most of the people you'll be dealing with won't care about your title. And unless you really do have associates, stay away from the "and Associates" tag.

- Get some advice on the legal and tax implications of operating as a contract worker or small business owner. Find a tax accountant who is experienced in this area. There are different options for running a business, from incorporating to operating as a sole proprietor. You should be aware of the pros and cons of each of these.

- Decide on where you are going to operate your business. At home, from an office, out of a business centre, sharing an office, or a combination of these?

- What will you use as your business address on your stationery and marketing materials?

- Set up your communications network. Your business phone number, fax number, email address, pager number, cell phone number. Decide whether you need a website or a PDF to market yourself, and set those up. Your telecommunications provider offers lots of options today to make you look and operate like a professional even if you operate from home. Familiarize yourself with these options and use them. Make sure that the telecommunications and Internet service providers you use are well established and reliable and, most importantly, will be there to help you if you have problems. They'll all tell you of course that they provide wonderful service. Try to find someone who uses them and ask them what their experience was when they had a problem. Make sure that the voice mail message on your main telephone number is businesslike and professional. Understand that when potential employers or clients respond to your marketing efforts, this is often the first impression they get of you, so develop the message accordingly.

Don't go the cheap route on these things. Saving yourself a couple of dollars a month could cost you much more in the long run. Be especially careful with the Internet service provider you choose. This is still a relatively new area and there are new companies starting up all the time. They're not all going to survive, so pick one that you're confident will be around in the future and that has a reputation for providing good service.

- Create your twenty-first century résumé and have some sample cover and marketing letters ready to use. Create everything in electronic form, including your brochure, and try them out on some of your contacts. It's easy to make changes when they're in this format, before you actually get them printed.

- Don't just pick people who are your big fans; pick others who are likely to give you honest and critical feedback. That's what you need. The better the job you do in this phase, the higher your chances of success when you go live with prospective clients or customers.

- Once you have thoroughly tested everything in electronic form, you can now move to the printed copy stage. Order your stationery and make sure that your business cards, letterhead, and envelopes have a consistent format. Order your brochure and any other marketing documents you want to use. Even though you've tested all of this stuff in electronic form, expect to make some changes after your initial printing, so don't commit to any volume at this point.

- Once you have all of your material ready, again test it before going live. Try it out on a cross-section of the contacts in your network. Send them the material as if they were prospects that you were going after and ask them for some critical feedback.

- Finally, before you go live, send your material out to your network and let them know that you're ready for business and request their help to get you up and running.

- If you think it is appropriate, get the word out to your peers or community on any blogs or social networks that you belong to.

- From the free publicity resources that are available to you, select the ones that you feel will be most beneficial to you and get the word out to them that you're ready for business.

Start your engines

Now that you've thoroughly tested all of your marketing materials, you're ready to get serious about finding work. You should always have your marketing materials with you in case you run into an acquaintance or a potential employer.

- Select five companies that you would like to work with. Given all the work you've done up to this point, you've probably identified some companies that you're itching to contact.

- Decide on how you are going to contact them, what you are going to say and what you want them to do. Be ready to answer questions about how much you charge and your payment terms. Are you prepared to offer any of these people a free, trial period to show them what you can do? How are you going to contact them?

    By telephone?

    By email?

    By fax?

By regular mail?

By popping in to see them?

If you opt for contact by email, fax, or regular mail, tell them that you will follow up with a phone call within a week and make sure you do that.

Finally, be on your toes and be ready to respond to inquiries from your marketing efforts. Be aware of what you've said in your marketing materials and be ready to back it up. From the moment you send this material out, assume that you're going to be contacted by telephone, email, or on your PDA, and respond in an appropriate manner.

Fine-tune your approach

It will take some time for you to contact all of these potential employers or clients. Once you've contacted all of them, take a step back and analyze how the whole experience went. What worked? What didn't work? Some of your marketing materials may need to be modified regardless of the testing you did previously.

You've taken the plunge into the deep end and now, like any other contractor or business that's just started up, you keep at it and keep modifying your approach until you get it right. Stay flexible and don't get discouraged. Nobody gets it right the first time, not even the big companies with all of the resources they have available to them. Welcome to the twenty-first-century workplace.

Final thoughts

Most of us were brought up, educated, and trained for a workplace that is fundamentally different from the one we see today and the one we will live with from now on. This transformation that is going on in the workplace presents challenges to the growing number of people who no longer have a job-centred career. To meet these challenges, we need to incorporate some survival techniques into our lives and keep a proper sense of perspective. Here are some things to consider.

Get regular exercise

Unlike our ancestors, most of us don't get enough exercise. Make a commitment to increase your physical fitness. The best way to do that is to join a fitness club and have them design a program for you. That way, you're more likely to stay with it and you'll be less likely to overdo it and injure yourself.

Keep mentally fit

- Make a point of reading uplifting, positive material.

- Avoid negative-thinking people and negative-oriented media.

- If you don't have a spiritual anchor, i.e., yoga, meditation, religion, etc., try to find one. We all get down at times and need something to calm us and lift our spirits.

Polish your communication skills

This is something that we all need to do; there's always room for improvement here. Actors, television broadcasters, and commentators are always sharpening their communication skills and we need to do the same.

Continue to grow

Push yourself and periodically check up on yourself to review what you have learned in recent weeks or months. What areas of your personal and working life need to be improved upon? What educational or training opportunities are coming up in the next few months that you plan to take advantage of?

Take some risks

Let your hair down now and then and try something new. Don't always look for answers from the so-called experts; trust your own judgement and experiment. Don't be afraid to fall on your face. That's how you learn and grow.

Say no more often

Live a balanced life. Our society is one of people frantically running around with never enough time for themselves or their families. That's the society that we've created and it's up to us to realize how wrong it is and to start to change it. Get your priorities straight. Family, health, personal, and spiritual values are far more important than business success. If you find that work is dominating your life, put on the brakes and get some of the work out of your life.

Try looking back

We get so wrapped up in our current and short-term challenges that our perspective on life gets out of balance. Most of our parents and grandparents went through some very tough times in their lives, tougher than what we are facing. They survived and moved on. So will you.

Be kind to yourself

It's a quirk of human nature that when we go through challenging times we occasionally get down on ourselves. Instead of beating yourself up, remind yourself of your successes. Learn the great art of doing the best you can with what you have and where you are. Good luck to you.

5
GUIDELINES FOR POST-SECONDARY STUDENTS

The true task of the individual is to rise to his or her own highest level of development as a human being, inspiring others to do the same.

— *Carol Orsborn, How Would Confucius Ask for a Raise?*

Getting Ready

Overview

By now you're well aware that you're heading into a workplace that's a much different place than the one your parents and grandparents made their living in. This isn't a temporary change that's been sparked by a slowdown in world economies. It's much more fundamental than that.

What you see in the workplace now is what you'll see throughout your career. The workplace of your parents and grandparents is gone and it won't be coming back, regardless of what happens in the economy. You'll have to be more diligent, creative, and strategic than they were just to find the work opportunities that exist. And you'll have to be much better at selling yourself than they were.

To add to all the tools and strategies you've been given so far, this section is devoted specifically to the needs of college/university students and will give you a complete arsenal of tools to succeed.

Common mistakes by students

- *Failing to plan ahead.* One of the most common mistakes college/university students continue to make is leaving the issue of finding work until the end of their final year or after they've graduated. That is an outdated approach that's inappropriate for today's workplace. At a minimum you need to address this issue at the beginning of your final year. Better still would be to develop a strategy throughout your college/university years, one that you sharpen as you look for work each summer.

- *Failing to use their Career Services or Student Employment Services departments.* You should be using these services throughout your college/university years to get ready for today's challenging workplace. You need to take advantage of all the resources available on campus to help you find work. Some of these departments offer excellent seminars, guidance counselling and other services and resources, yet the percentage of students who take advantage of them is minimal. And this is a universal problem. As per the first point, sometimes students show up at these departments just before they graduate or after they graduate. Some alumni associations offer these services too, but again, few grads take advantage of them. Many people who are already in the workplace regret not seeking career advice at the beginning of their careers. According to a January 2006 poll by Ipsos-Reid, two-thirds of working Canadians wish they had sought more career-planning advice when they were starting out. You need to set yourself a goal of finding meaningful work before you graduate. If you haven't been using these services throughout your college/university years, rectify that by visiting them right at the beginning of your final year. Make sure you know about all the seminars they offer and the services available to you and take advantage of them. Tell the people there that you've set a goal of finding work before you graduate and ask for their help to achieve that goal. They'll be happy to assist you. That's what they're there for.

- *Having poor communication and presentation skills.* One would think that people able to graduate from college or university would be smart enough and professional enough not to send out résumés or CVs with spelling and grammatical errors. But apparently not, according to the recruiters, hiring managers, and employers who receive them. They say that they regularly receive résumés or CVs from college/university grads that have these errors. Sometimes they receive résumés or CVs that are impressive and show the type of background they're looking for, which prompts them to go to the next step in the hiring process and contact the student to come in for an interview. Problem is, when they do contact them, the student doesn't recognize their name or the name of their company, which obviously creates a poor first impression. Another complaint is that while the résumé or CV may be impressive, the way the student comes across on the telephone when they contact them is anything but impressive. As one recruiter put it, "Although their résumé is great, their phone manner sinks them." Getting too fancy by creating résumés or CVs with Photoshop and going overboard on the design end is another mistake. Bottom line? The minimum standard you need to meet is to create marketing tools that are businesslike and error-free. And if recruiters, hiring managers, or employers contact you by telephone, you must be ready to back up what you said in the material you sent to them and of course immediately recognize who they are and the name of their company.

- *Being focused on a "job."* You need to broaden your view of earning a living and be prepared to accept contract work. This option is often regarded as inferior by our backwards-looking society. However, it may well be a better option for you and may open up more employment opportunities. Most opportunities today are found in small companies. If the only option you give these employers is to offer you a "job," you're making it hard for them to hire you. When you graduate, your priority should be to get experience in the field you want to work in, and being willing to accept contract work, without reservations, is an attitude you need to develop. You need to understand that many of the students who end up with good jobs got them because of the experience they picked up as contract workers. And there's no surety that someone will offer you a job. You may need to create your own job. That doesn't mean you have to start a business, though that may be an option that appeals to you. You can create your own job by offering your services on a contract basis, especially to small companies. The British management guru Charles Handy predicted about ten years ago that increasingly, people would earn their living from "Portfolio Careers," i.e., from several part-time occupations rather than a full-time job. The Electronic Recruiting Exchange reports that as many as a third of new workers are looking for alternatives to full-time employment.

- *Putting too much emphasis on joining large companies.* This might be reinforced by the fact that large companies still dominate the typical job fair at our colleges and universities. The people responsible for these fairs need to do more to attract small companies to them, because that's where most of the action is. Students underestimate the competition for jobs with large companies. Recruiters from these companies who visit campuses are often overwhelmed by applications from students. Getting well over 100 applications for each position they want to fill is common. According to a May 2005 poll by Robert Half International, on average, only five applicants for each job opening are interviewed. The point here is not to discourage you from applying with large companies. If that's what you want, go for it, but don't get frustrated and depressed if they don't hire you. There are lots of other options out there. And getting back to the point that your priority should be to focus on getting experience in your field: Sometimes you can get more hands-on and practical experience with a small company. There's less chance of you being pigeonholed into a narrow slot with a small company than is the case with a large one.

Essential skills for students

- *Be crystal clear about the skill set you have to offer potential employers and how it will benefit them.* This is key. Yet many students fail to understand this. The typical résumé or CV received by recruiters, hiring managers, and employers portrays the individual in a general way and is not tailored to the needs of the company. Your parents could get away with that approach; you can't. Their résumé or CV was probably received by the company's personnel or human resources department, and the people there had the luxury of taking the time to determine if the applicant's skill set could be useful to their company. That's all changed. The company you'll be applying to may not have a personnel or human resources department. Screening applications will be one of many hats the recipient will be wearing, and occupying several roles at any one time is typical in today's multi-tasking world. They don't have the time to determine if the skill set you have to offer will benefit them or not. That's your job, not theirs. The only résumés, CVs, and other marketing materials they receive that will get their initial attention are the ones that show that the applicant has done some research on the company and that clearly spell out how their background and skill set can potentially help the company.

- *Know how to find hidden work opportunities.* Most people who understand today's workplace agree that the majority of employment opportunities, at least 80 percent of them, are never advertised. Yet many students' strategy for finding work, like most employment seekers, is to focus on what is advertised — in newspapers, on Internet job sites, and at careers fairs. That's because this approach is nice and easy; there's no risk involved. Assuming you have the skill set the company needs, they're asking you to submit your application. Students, again like most employment seekers, often have an aversion to approaching companies that are not advertising. They reason that if the company isn't advertising, they're not hiring, which isn't true at all. Recruiters, hiring managers, and employers all know that trying to find employees through conventional advertising is one of the least effective ways to accomplish this, and increasingly they're staying away from it. That's why they're turning to Employee Referral Programs (see Chapter 1), posting jobs on their own websites, and using other non-traditional ways of finding employees. If you're one of the many who have an aversion to contacting companies unless you see them advertising that they're hiring, you need to change your thinking. Many of them are hiring; they're simply not advertising that fact in the traditional, conventional way. You need to develop a strategy that will let you tap into the hidden job market as was described in Chapter 1 of the book. Spend 90 percent of your time strategizing around which companies are likely to be interested in your skill set and how you're going to contact them. Spend the other 10 percent of your time getting your marketing materials out to them and following up with them. Never resort to the most common approach used by employment seekers of sending out lots of résumés or CVs in a shotgun manner. It doesn't work, and you'll only end up frustrated and discouraged if you do this.

- *Know how to find work in a more comprehensive and strategically effective way than the average employment seeker does.* Showing you how to do that is what this book is all about. Employment seekers typically use one tool only, a traditional résumé or CV. You need to develop all the tools I describe in the book and know how to use them. Sample marketing tools for college/university students are provided in this section, and you can use these and the other samples in the book in developing your own tools. And make sure you use all of the strategies outlined in the book in your search for work.

- *Become an active and effective networker.* I cover this topic extensively in this book because it is such an essential skill. Almost all of the people who are finding the good jobs and interesting, meaningful work today are effective networkers. But this isn't something that you should address after you graduate. On the contrary, it's a skill you should be developing throughout your college/university years. And there are lots of opportunities for you to do that. On campus there are many clubs, special interest groups, and other groups that you can get involved with and begin to develop networking skills. There may well be a need for a new group, one that you could either start up on your own or with other students who share your interest in a particular area. You can network online by being part of an appropriate blog or social network. You may be able to tap into useful information about the field you want to work in and get feedback from people who already work in it from these sources. There certainly are lots of opportunities for you to network off campus. Instead of waiting for employers to show up for the annual career fair at your college or university, why not get a head start on your competition by meeting some of these people at the professional association meetings, conferences, and trade shows going on in your area? Some professional associations offer student memberships. Check out the associations related to the field you want to work in to see if they offer student memberships. Check out their upcoming meeting topics, and if one of them is on an area of particular interest to you, make a point of attending it. If they don't have student memberships but you'd like to attend one of their meetings, contact them anyway and they'll probably accommodate you. At these meetings you will meet some of the "players" in your field, pick up information about what is going on and maybe even sniff out some employment opportunities that will never be advertised.

- *Be able to sell yourself confidently and effectively.* I devote a lot of attention in this book to debunking the stereotypical views on what selling is all about. If you have any lingering thoughts that you're not good at selling yourself, you need to get rid of them. In many respects, the point of all the work you've been doing so far is to build up your confidence by making you aware of how today's workplace operates and to show you how to succeed in it. It's important that you understand that the payoff for doing all this work is that you are light-years ahead of the average employment seeker. You will be pleasantly surprised at the results of your search for work and your effectiveness in interviews. The common view of what selling is about is pure bunk. The "gift of the gab" is not an asset — it's a liability. The people you want to connect with are not waiting for you to show up and give them a sales pitch — that's the last thing they want. People who don't see themselves as the stereotypical sales type sometimes use that as an excuse for not putting themselves out in the marketplace and taking some risks. So they stick with the safe but ineffective approach of applying only for positions that are advertised. If you are a low-key individual, be assured that many of the people who are very successful in sales are like that too. There's no such thing as a born salesman or saleswoman. Successful salespeople achieved their success through working hard, believing in the product or service they sell, knowing it inside out, knowing how it can benefit potential customers, and by not being easily discouraged. By having the fortitude to stay with your studies throughout your college or university years and by graduating, you've already shown that you've got what it takes to succeed in sales and in life.

You and the Internet

As pointed out in Chapter 3, people who regularly use the Internet often don't realize that they're creating an online persona. Students, who are generally heavy users of the Internet, need to pay attention to this issue. Remember when you're blogging, posting information on a social network, or entering information about yourself online that it's not only your friends and peers who will see this information. It is available to anyone who chooses to look for it.

If you understand this, you will think twice about entering information on any source on the Internet that could create a negative impression about you. Even your email address could send out the wrong signal about you. Some students have an email address, particularly through Hotmail and Yahoo!, that is designed to be seen as cool, funny, or outrageous by their friends and peers. A potential employer may see it in an entirely different light. To them, you might come across as immature and unprofessional.

It's not that they're a bunch of party-poopers with no sense of humor. All they know about you is what they see on your résumé/CV or on the Internet. Views you've expressed or comments you've made that you thought were quite innocent and not intended to be offensive may raise questions about your judgment. Potential employers have no way of assessing whether what they are seeing is intended to be a joke or is an accurate reflection of you and the type of person you are. A question that is always on their mind is, "Would this person fit within the culture of our organization?"

While they could give you the benefit of the doubt, the fact is that they typically have lots of choices and they may just pass on you if they come across anything that could be seen as contentious or that raises questions about your maturity and attitude.

Perhaps you've been applying for lots of jobs that you have no doubt you're qualified for and have not been getting any replies. Or you've been getting interviews that you thought went really well, but you never hear anything further from the employer. These may be red flags for you to pay attention to. You may need to give serious thought to the final question posed at the end of Chapter 3, i.e., "What would a search on the Internet reveal about you?"

Creating a financial plan

Our society doesn't appreciate how much we take for granted when we have a steady traditional job. People who unexpectedly lose their job learn this the hard way. Some of the financial things they often take for granted include the following:

- being paid on a regular basis, typically every two weeks
- being paid for working overtime
- being paid during vacation times
- getting annual pay increases
- possibly getting bonuses throughout the year
- having their employer pay into their pension plan
- having their benefit plan include extended health care coverage
- having a benefit plan including life insurance
- having a benefit plan including long-term disability payments in the event of an accident or illness that prevents them from working
- having their family's health care needs covered
- having their employer help to pay, in whole or in part, for continuing education courses they're taking

The reality many of these people have to face is that they'll have to accept contract work, or part-time/temporary work, where some and possibly all of these things are not included. Further, they may have to accept the fact that they will earn less than they did when they had a steady job.

One could argue that it has always made sense to have a financial plan, but the fact is, many people don't have one. If they have a steady job right up until they retire, not having a financial plan might not be that significant because of all the benefits and coverage that comes with their job.

With an increasing number of students earning a living outside of the traditional steady job, not having a financial plan could have serious repercussions. Add to this the fact that many students today are starting their working lives handicapped by student loans and significant credit card debt.

You need to give this issue a lot more thought than your parents and grandparents did, assuming they made their living from a traditional steady job. You would be wise to take advantage of any seminars, courses, or counselling that may be available to you at your college or university on this topic. If nothing is available, you should meet with a financial advisor and create a plan for yourself. Also acquaint yourself with the tax regulations in your country that apply to people who earn their living as contract workers, consultants, or through any other form of self-employment.

You don't want to get any nasty surprises when it comes to preparing your income tax statement at the end of the year. Make sure you know about all of the expenses you may deduct from your earnings, and keep track of them during the year. Also, ask yourself what health care coverage you have in the event of an accident or a long-term illness. What if you need some extensive dental work, new eyeglasses, physiotherapy, or other such treatment?

Finally, realize that unlike many of your parents and grandparents, a pension at the end of your working life may only be available if it is something you have provided for and contributed to throughout your career, as part of your financial plan.

Action plan

- Increase your fitness level, both physically and mentally, by following the suggestions in Chapter 4 of the book.

- Join a Toastmasters International group or start one.

- Create a "work-search" group of your peers who are serious about finding meaningful and rewarding work and who are prepared to invest the time to make that happen. Set up regular meeting times, encourage and prod one another, and monitor each other's progress in the goal of finding work *before* you graduate. To achieve that goal, all of your marketing tools must be complete by the end of January in your final year, *at the latest.* Also, you need to be ready to start sending out your marketing material to prospective employers by the end of February, *at the latest.*

- The first thing everybody in your group has to do is describe to the others the type of work they're looking for and where they think they'll find it. Everybody in the group has to be clear on this before going any further. Ask for some feedback from your career counsellors on this.

- Create a "Workplace Activity Database" for the industry sectors you would like to work in. In it will be all the latest information on developments and trends in that sector that you can get from trade journals, industry and professional associations, websites, newsletters, and any networking events going on in your area. It's imperative that you be on top of what's going on in these sectors. Ask the staff in your college library for help in getting this information. While you're at the library, find out if they offer any seminars or instruction on how to do basic research on companies, both on the Internet and using more traditional media. Being competent at this is an essential skill you need to acquire (if you haven't already). Once you have this information, share it with your group and explain to them how it affects your plans to market yourself to employers in that sector.

- From all the work you did in Chapter 2 of the book, you've already determined your marketable skills and how you see those helping the employers you plan to contact. Get feedback on this from your group and your career counsellors. Understand that from a prospective employer's perspective, the key question will be "How will hiring this person make my life easier?" If you stay focused on that, you'll be miles ahead of the typical work seeker, who rarely considers it.

- Get some personalized stationery, i.e., matching business cards, letterhead and envelopes. The major office supply stores offer these in packages in a variety of formats. These are inexpensive but professional-looking and are perfectly adequate to meet your marketing goals. Don't be tempted to get fancy here with expensive stationery, which won't impress anyone.

- Before you order your stationery, you'll have to determine your communications network. See Chapter 4 of the book for how to do this. Make sure that the voice mail on your main telephone number is businesslike. You'll be investing a lot of effort into marketing yourself, so make sure that when potential employers respond, they won't be put off by some goofy message that may get a laugh from your peers but won't impress these people.

- Start to develop your marketing tools as described in Chapter 3 of the book. Pay particular attention to marketing letters; they could be your most effective tool in finding work. See the sample marketing letter for grads that follows this section and the other sample marketing tools for grads.

- As you develop your marketing tools, test them for effectiveness via email with your group and fine-tune them before you send them out to employers. You should also show them to your career counsellors to get their feedback.

- From your Workplace Activity Database, identify any networking events coming up in your area and make a point of attending them, armed with your new marketing tools.

- From all the work you've been doing, hopefully you have identified some companies you'd like to work with. Make a list of five of these. Tell your group and career counsellors why you've selected these companies and what you feel you have to offer them, then get their feedback.

- Determine what marketing tools you feel are appropriate to send to these same companies, e.g., a marketing letter, a cover letter, and a twenty-first century résumé, or a cover letter and a brochure. Mention in your letters to employers that you'll follow up with them within a week and make sure you do that.

- After you've contacted all five employers, take some time to review the results and discuss them with your group and career counsellors. What did you learn? Do you need to make some changes to your marketing tools and how you're approaching employers?

- If you don't find work in your first attempt, don't be discouraged. Your efforts will pay off; you can be sure of that. If you do find work, share the good news with your group and career counsellors and continue to work with and support those in your group who have yet to find work. Good luck.

Sample marketing letter for grads

Put yourself in the place of a typical employer who constantly receives unsolicited, traditional résumés in the mail. Each arrives in a brown envelope with a hand-written address and return address. After a while employers recognize such an envelope as a résumé, even before they open it. There's a good chance, therefore, that they won't open it; they'll put it straight into the garbage. They're not being rude. They just don't have the time to look at it.

Now assume they received the marketing letter (See Sample 10) in a professional-looking envelope, with a printed label, and inside is matching letterhead and a business card. Right off the bat the sender has created a positive impression.

In the letter they see that the sender knows something about them and their industry and feels they have something to offer them. Which of these two approaches do you think is likely to get a response from that employer? Even if they don't need the services of the grad who is offering them, you can be sure they'll remember that grad when they follow up with them by telephone.

Another advantage of this approach is that it addresses an issue that makes many people uncomfortable, "cold-calling."

Instead of calling a prospective employer out of the blue and interrupting what they're doing, you have a legitimate reason for calling them. You're doing what you said you would do in your marketing letter, following up, and they will know who you are. That makes both parties more comfortable and changes the call to what is known in sales as a "warm call" instead of a "cold call."

When you do follow up with employers, if they don't need your services, there's a good chance you'll get a favorable response because of your professional approach. If you do, that's the time to ask them politely if they're aware of any companies that might be hiring. Don't be shy about doing this. Employers won't be offended by it.

Sample 10
MARKETING LETTER FOR GRADS

189–2186 Brownstone Avenue

Vancouver, BC V8M 2J6

Phone: (604) 555-9999, Email: rmg@istar.ca

Date: _____

Dear _____

You will not notice when writing is good, but you will notice when writing is bad.

Today, more than ever, clear communication is necessary for survival in business.

With increased access to information and competing — often conflicting — messages, people are becoming frustrated with what they see, read, and hear. Making sure your message is quickly and easily understood is imperative.

I graduate this May from _____ with a major in communications. I have experience in the preparation of:

* Business plans   * Reports

* Technical writing   * Training manuals

* Product literature   * Advertising copy

* Press releases/news articles   * Feature articles

I have strong skills in both Mac and Windows operating systems. I work equally well on my own or as part of a team. I am open to contract and full-time employment.

I have studied your website and the sites of a couple of your competitors and I have a few ideas that may interest you. Whether in print or onscreen, I will bring your words to life. I will follow up with you by telephone within a week, or please feel free to contact me at (604) 555-9999 or by email at rmg@istar.ca

Sincerely,

Rose M. Gerty

Since you obviously put a fair amount of effort into your letter to them, they'll be impressed by that.

Sample twenty-first century résumé for grads

Like the sample twenty-first century résumé given earlier in the book, keep your résumé to one page (See Sample 11). The objective of the résumé is to get a potential employer's attention and have them contact you, not give them your whole life story, as many résumés attempt to do.

You may want to create a more detailed résumé if you have a lot of experience. Take it along with you if you are called for an interview and, if you think it helps your cause, offer it to your prospective employer.

Under "Experience" you can include any co-op experience you picked up at college or university or any experience you have obtained as a volunteer, if you think it is relevant. You may have worked on projects at college or university that may be of interest to a potential employer. You may even have had some exposure to leading-edge technologies or research that could be of interest to a potential employer.

You need to create an effective cover letter to accompany your résumé. See the example given earlier in the book. You will of course show these letters to your "work-search" group and career counsellors for feedback before you send them out.

Sample brochure for grads

Like the previous sample brochure in the book, Sample 12 one is only intended to give you the gist of how to create a brochure. In reality, this text is what you would give to a printer or graphics designer to have them dress it up and create a professional-looking brochure.

Don't be tempted to get fancy with glossy paper and heavy use of graphics; that isn't necessary and will only increase the expense. Stay with standard printer colors and print stock. "Simple and businesslike" should be the format of your brochure.

It is very important that you get feedback from your work-search group on your brochure before you get it printed. Coming up with effective rhetorical questions on side one will take time and practice.

TWENTY-FIRST CENTURY RÉSUMÉ FOR GRADS

Rose M. Gerty

A communications professional with strong skills on Mac and Windows systems. Experienced in writing technical material, advertising copy, press releases, news articles, and training manuals.

Experience

Worked on a contract basis for an established Vancouver software company to upgrade and improve the quality of their product literature.

Worked for a ministry of the British Columbia government for a summer as a writer, improving the readability and effectiveness of their training manuals, which are used in their offices throughout British Columbia.

Work on a continuing, part-time basis for an advertising company as a writer/editor of advertising copy, press releases, and feature articles.

Work History

Effective Advertising Services, Vancouver, BC, 2000–2003   www.eas.ca
Part-Time Writer/Editor

BC Ministry of Human Resources, Summer 2002
Technical Writer

Superior Business Software, Vancouver, BC, Summer 2001   www.sbsw.ca
Writer/Editor

Education

Bachelor of Arts, English Literature, Simon Fraser University (expected in 2004)

189–2186 Brownstone Avenue, Vancouver, BC V8M 2J6
Phone: (604) 555-9999 / Email: rmg@istar.ca

BROCHURE FOR GRADS

Side One

Rose M. Gerty

A communications professional with strong skills on Mac and Windows systems. Experienced in writing technical material, advertising copy, press releases, news articles, and training manuals.

Ž Would you like to improve the quality of the product literature you send out to your customers?

Ž Would you like to improve the readability and effectiveness of your website?

Ž Do you need help with press releases and feature articles about your products and services?

Ž Do your training manuals need to be upgraded and improved?

If you answered yes to any of these questions, I can help you at rates you can afford.

You can reach me at:
(604) 555-9999 or
rmg@istar.ca

Whether in print or onscreen,
I will bring your words to life.

Side Two

Rose M. Gerty
Sample Projects

Ž Revised, upgraded, and improved the product literature for an established software company.

Ž Upgraded and improved the readability of training manuals for a British Columbia government ministry.

Ž Wrote press releases and feature articles for a communications consulting company.

Ž Worked with an advertising company as a writer/editor on advertising copy and promotional material.

You can reach me at:
(604) 555-9999 or
rmg@istar.ca

Whether in print or on-screen,
I will bring your words to life.

Having a brochure comes in very handy when you attend networking events, and it makes you stand out from the masses who are still depending on traditional résumés. It also makes you look more professional.

Always carry your brochures with you and distribute them among the people in your network. They're more likely to pass on your brochure to someone they think might be interested in hiring you than they are to pass on your résumé.

Even if you don't plan to have brochures printed up, the exercise of creating one is beneficial to you psychologically, in that it forces you to pinpoint exactly what you have to offer and how that benefits potential employers. It also forces you to anticipate the types of challenges potential employers might have that you can help them with, and this will make you much more effective in an interview.

Sample website for grads

The first thing you will notice about the sample website in Sample 13 is its similarity to the sample brochure. That is as it should be: You're simply presenting the same information in a different format.

As with your brochure, don't be tempted to get fancy with your website. "Simple and businesslike" are the main guidelines in putting it together. Stay away from the "flash and splash" type of format with heavy use of graphics. Such bells and whistles aren't necessary and may even turn some people off.

The example here would consist of three simple pages, which is perfectly adequate for the majority of people. As with your brochure, get some feedback on your website from your work-search group and others in your network before you distribute it.

Finally, make sure your website is technically complete and functional. It is counterproductive to go to the trouble of creating a website if it contains broken links or other technical glitches. This will create a poor impression and raise questions about your ability to produce quality work.

Sample 13
WEBSITE FOR GRADS

Rose M. Gerty

189 – 2186 Brownstone Ave., Vancouver, BC V8M 2J6
Tel: (604) 555-9999 / Email: rmg@istar.ca www.rmg.ca

A communications professional with strong skills on Mac and Windows systems.	Contact
Experienced in writing technical materials, advertising copy, press releases, news articles, and training manuals.	Samples
Would you like to improve the quality of the product literature you send out to your customers?	Info

A communications professional with strong skills on Mac and
Windows systems.

Experienced in writing technical materials, advertising copy,
press releases, news articles, and training manuals.

*Would you like to improve the quality of the product literature
you send out to your customers?*

*Would you like to improve the readability and effectiveness of
your website?*

*Do you need help with press releases and feature articles about
your products and services?*

Do your training manuals need to be upgraded and improved?

If you answered yes to any of these questions, I can help you at
rates you can afford.

Whether in print or onscreen, I will bring your words to life.

Contact

Samples

Info

SELF-COUNSEL PRESS — HOW TO FIND WORK IN THE 21ST CENTURY 09

6
CAREER COUNSELLING IN SECONDARY SCHOOLS

Tell me, I'll forget. Show me, I may remember. But involve me, and I'll understand.

— *Chinese Proverb*

Twenty-first Century Career Counselling

Career counselling has never been a high priority within our education system, at either the secondary or post-secondary level. Further, in times of budget restraint, it is often first on the list of items eligible for cutbacks.

Yet if the administrators, bureaucrats, and politicians who are responsible for funding and managing our education system really understood how much the workplace has changed, career counselling would be given a much higher priority than it has ever had in the past. It's not that they don't care about the challenges their students are facing in entering today's workplace. They do care. But they can't relate, because they have no experience in it themselves.

The workplace they graduated into was vastly different to what it is today. In those days, anyone graduating from a college or university was almost guaranteed a decent job, and outplacement, re-engineering,

135

and outsourcing were terms that the average person had never heard of. Getting a traditional job that promised stable employment, included a benefit plan and offered a pension on retirement was a given. Had anyone suggested to graduates back then that they would have to take on part-time, temporary, or contract work, with no benefits or pension plan, they would have been laughed at.

As pointed out in Chapter 1 of the book, there are currently over 2,000 courses in entrepreneurship being offered in US colleges and universities, up from 253 in 1985. Also pointed out was the fact that many colleges and universities are hiring active or retired business owners to teach these courses rather than academics.

The politicians, bureaucrats, and administrators who fund and manage the secondary school sector should decide on the most effective way to educate their students about entrepreneurship and the challenges of self employment.

The fourth R

For decades we have talked about the three Rs of education: reading, writing, and arithmetic. The time has come to add a fourth R, running your own business: a concept that will cover all aspects of self-employment.

Considering how the workplace has changed and the very real possibility that secondary school graduates will at some point in their working lives earn their living through some form of self-employment, they should, at the very least, obtain a fundamental understanding of the challenges of self-employment. These students must acquire an entrepreneurial mentality about marketing themselves and about meeting the needs of employers. They must learn how to create marketing tools beyond the traditional résumé or CV that will get the attention of employers. Sample marketing tools for students are included in this section.

As part of their secondary school experience, these students must learn how to do basic research on companies, how to find hidden work opportunities, how to network effectively and how to sell themselves confidently and effectively. And it is up to the career counsellors to teach them these skills.

This is quite a challenge for career counsellors, since some of them have never had to apply these skills in their own careers. It requires a shift away from career counselling per se to more emphasis on showing students how to become more entrepreneurial or enterprising in their approach to finding work and to earning their living outside of the traditional full-time job.

Given how fundamentally the workplace has changed, the training secondary school career counsellors receive could probably benefit from a review to determine how appropriate that training is for today's workplace. In light of the changed workplace, it only makes sense that those entering the career counselling area should obtain some experience earning a living outside of the traditional job, so they can impart that knowledge to their students.

Today's secondary school graduates will have to be more diligent, creative, and strategic than their parents were just to find the work opportunities that exist, and they'll have to be better at selling themselves. It's thus common sense, and also in their own best interest, for people entering the career counselling area to acquire these skills themselves through direct experience.

These are exciting and challenging times for secondary school career counsellors and those responsible for funding and managing this area. The key question is: How does the typical secondary school elevate an area that historically has been a low priority to the much higher level it must operate at in order for their students to succeed in the new workplace?

There are no simple answers to this question. But a good starting point would be for all the people involved, directly or indirectly, with career counselling across the educational spectrum to recognize how much more important this field is today, to look for ways to make it more effective, and to allocate more resources to it.

Work centers

One way to make this field more effective would be to separate career counselling from the other area of helping students to find work and ensuring that they have the tools to succeed in today's workplace. Career counselling would deal with all the issues around helping students determine what type of work they should pursue or what area they should focus on, should they decide to pursue further education and training beyond secondary school, i.e., college, university, trade school, or self-employment.

Career counselling should be the place for students, and perhaps their parents, to go to get advice on what types of careers make sense for them, based on their abilities and interests, as determined through counselling and proven tests like the Myers-Briggs.

The "Work Center" would be the place where students who have moved beyond career counselling, and who know the type of work they want, would go to get practical advice on how to find work and succeed in that area. There, they would learn how to create marketing tools that are appropriate for today's workplace. They'd learn how to do basic research on the sector they want to work in, find hidden work opportunities, network effectively, and sell themselves confidently and successfully to employers. Those who want to pursue self-employment would be given advice and access to appropriate materials that would show them how to do this properly.

At the moment, of necessity, career counsellors are doing their best to cover both of these different areas. In future, it would make more sense to hire people who have the training and experience to provide help to students in one of these areas, but not both. While these people might still be classified as career counsellors, which area they were hired for would be determined by their training, experience, and preference.

The challenge for secondary-school career counsellors, today and tomorrow, is to show their students how to succeed in the workplace with a different set of tools and strategies than has been used in the past.

Co-op education

Those responsible for funding and managing our secondary schools would be doing their students a big favor if they made co-op education a mandatory part of the curriculum. It is probably the most significant and practical thing we can do to help our students get a good start in their working lives. The advantages of co-op education to the students cannot be overstated.

Integrating students' academic studies with relevant work experience gives them a chance to apply skills they learned in the classroom, making their education more relevant and practical. And students should be able to participate in co-op education programs regardless of the area they want to work in, e.g., the arts, health, non-profit, education, business, or any other sector that interests them.

Co-op education programs provide excellent opportunities for students to develop skills and abilities in their field of choice. On the job, students can build knowledge, develop business savvy and, in turn, gain confidence in their marketability. Such programs in secondary schools help to build bridges between the schools and employers, across the whole workplace spectrum. They also give employers an opportunity to provide direct feedback to the secondary schools on how effective their co-op education programs are and how they could be improved.

In today's workplace it makes absolute sense to strengthen ties between our educators and the employers who will ultimately hire their students. In preparing their students for the workplace, there's only so much educators can accomplish within the classroom or school. Extending students' education beyond the school and into the workplace makes their education so much more relevant and benefits everyone involved.

Building alliances

Significantly expanding the resources in the career counselling and co-op education areas will directly benefit secondary school students by enriching their education experience, building their self-confidence and increasing their chances of succeeding in whatever field they choose to work in.

These are valid reasons for allocating more resources to these areas, but, as a practical matter, it is questionable whether these alone would persuade the responsible bureaucrats and politicians to provide more funding. So a stronger business case will probably have to be developed in order to obtain that additional funding.

It is also questionable whether the staff and administrators in our secondary schools who are responsible for career counselling and co-op education can develop, on their own, the business case for increased funding. Their pitch for more funding may be seen as empire building, and even if it isn't, their request will be only one of many the bureaucrats and politicians have to consider from the various groups within the secondary school sector. So they will have to find ways to build a stronger, and more politically acceptable, business case.

One way to do that is to get support for additional funding from sources outside of the secondary schools. Groups such as Junior Achievement and Young Enterprise have a strong record of working with secondary schools to help their students succeed in the workplace. If they can be convinced of the benefits to students of increasing funding to career counselling and co-op education programs, and can be persuaded to actively support the idea, that will increase the chances of getting the additional funding.

Students are not the only ones who will benefit from this increased funding. The employers who hire them will benefit from it too. They will be getting students who are more motivated, mature, job-ready, and productive as a result of this increased funding. So, before staff and administrators in our secondary schools approach the bureaucrats and politicians for more funding, they should try to get as many groups across the workplace sector as possible to buy into the idea and to lend their support to it.

Chambers of commerce, professional associations, and all the other associations that represent the various sectors in the workplace should be approached and made aware of the advantages of this increased funding to their members who would be hiring the students, and to get their active support for the idea. Since most work opportunities today are to be found in small businesses, any associations that represent this sector should be contacted as well. Groups like the Canadian Federation of Independent Business (CFIB), the Small Firms Association of Ireland (SFA), and the Federation of Small Businesses (FSB) in the UK would be appropriate associations to contact.

Marketing tools for students

Following are sample marketing tools for secondary students that they, and the career counsellors, can use as a guide in developing their own marketing tools. They include a marketing letter, envelope, cover letter, twenty-first century résumé or CV, brochure, and website or PDF. The brochure and website or PDF are optional. However, career counsellors must ensure that their students know how to produce all of the other tools in a format that is visually pleasing and businesslike.

They're called marketing tools because they're used in the marketing phase of looking for work, as opposed to applying for a job. Students will use these when they're marketing themselves to employers on speculation and trying to get their attention. A traditional résumé or CV, along with a cover letter, is the tool they would use to apply for a job that has been advertised and for which they feel they are qualified.

Sample marketing letter for students

Have your students create letterhead as shown at the top of Sample 14 that they will use for all correspondence with potential employers. It will contain their name, address, and contact information in an organized and businesslike format. Also, tell them to use white, standard paper only when they create their marketing tools, no colored or fancy paper.

Give them lots of practice to ensure that they know how to create a document that is organized, businesslike, and visually appealing, using MS Word or a similar software package. Tell them to use the spell-checking feature of the software, and if they have any doubt at all about the spelling of the name of the individual they're sending the letter to, they need to verify it.

This marketing letter is sent on its own, with no résumé attached, in an envelope with a printed address label and a printed return address label. A sample envelope is included in this section. Remember, students are not applying for a job; they're in the marketing mode. The objective of the marketing letter is to arouse the interest of the person they're sending it to. Note that the letter quickly establishes that they're open to part-time, full-time, or contract work in an entry-level position.

It goes on to establish that they have some experience in their industry and familiarity with some of the software that is commonly used in that industry. It also establishes the fact that they have taken the time to look at the company's website and that they know something about the type of work the company does. It furthermore states that the individual is reliable, hard-working, and that they can provide references from companies they've worked for to back up this claim. This will appeal to most employers.

MARKETING LETTER FOR STUDENTS

420 Pape Avenue   **Chuck Carr (416) 555-6666**
Toronto, ON M3S 1C5   **cjcarr50@hotmail.com**

May 7, 2007

Dear Mr. Lonergan,

I will be graduating from Leaside High School next month and I'm looking for an entry-level position in the Graphics Design industry. I am willing to work on a part-time, full-time, or contract basis.

I have experience with Adobe Photoshop, Illustrator, and InDesign. I got that experience during my final year at Leaside High School, when I worked for the Shell Graphics and Design company of Toronto on a co-op education basis.

I have experience working with both Mac and Windows operating systems, and I've used most of the popular business software packages both at Shell Graphics & Design and in my computer classes at Leaside High School.

I've looked at your website, and some of the sample work you list there is similar to what I worked on at Shell Graphics & Design.

My references from Shell Graphics & Design and the other companies where I have worked part-time during my years at Leaside High School show that I am a reliable and hardworking individual.

I am willing to work for you for a week without pay to show you what I can do. I will be following up with you by telephone within the next week or, if it is more convenient for you, please contact me at either the telephone number or email address shown above.

Sincerely,

Chuck Carr

SELF-COUNSEL PRESS — HOW TO FIND WORK IN THE 21ST CENTURY 09

At the end, the student could make an offer to work for the company for a week for free to show them what they can do. This is optional, but it is something that will impress and appeal to some employers. It also works for the student in that it would give them a chance to see if this is an environment and type of company that they would like to work for before making a long-term commitment. Also, at the end, the student makes a commitment to follow up with the employer by telephone within a week and gives the employer, politely, the option to contact the student.

Marketing letters can be a very effective tool to get the attention of potential employers and open up a positive dialogue with them, so give your students plenty of practice in creating them, until you're convinced that they clearly understand what these tools are all about and are comfortable creating them.

Sample envelope

Many of the résumés or CVs that recruiters, hiring managers and employers receive come in a standard 8½ by 11 inch brown envelope, with the recipient's name and address and the return address handwritten. This makes them stand out from other correspondence, which generally has a printed address label and a printed return address label or the sender's logo and address printed at the top left.

Recipients instinctively know when they receive such a brown envelope that it's probably a résumé or CV from someone and therefore, in today's busy work environment, they might just toss it into the garbage. They're not being rude; they just don't have the time to look at it, and besides, most of these résumés or CVs are unsolicited, so they are under no obligation to look at them.

If they receive an envelope as shown in Sample 15, there's a better chance that they'll actually open it, versus the hand-written ones they receive. When they do open it, if nothing else, they see a document that is visually attractive and that shows that the sender has taken some care in creating it. So the sender has created a positive first impression. They may be even further impressed when they see that it is from a high school student, given the amateurish documents they typically receive from students.

Sample 15
ENVELOPE

Chuck Carr
420 Pape Avenue
Toronto, ON M3S 1C5

                Mr. E. Lonergan
                Xulu Graphics
                65 Carlton Street
                Toronto, ON M5T 2G4

Impress on your students the importance of sending out their documents to employers in this way. The address label and return address label are standard stock that can be purchased from any office supplies outlet. Software packages such as Word are set up to print these labels, so make sure your students know how to create them.

Sample cover letter for students

Many employment seekers fail to understand the significance of a carefully crafted cover letter. Most of them rarely get past the "Dear Sir, please find attached" style and format, which is ineffective. Such a letter must get straight to the point and never waste the recipient's time with generalities, like the example in Sample 16.

Some of the elements you would include in a marketing letter need to be in a cover letter. It must complement and enhance the résumé or CV that is attached. The content must be positive and upbeat, but in an effective rather than in an insincere or pushy way. The letter must quickly establish the fact that the sender knows something about the company and that they feel they have a skill set and/or experience that might be of interest and benefit to the company.

The length should be one page only and a short one page at that. The objective of the cover letter is to get the recipient interested enough in the sender to go on and look at the résumé/CV that is attached. To do that, it must be marketing oriented, tailored to the needs of the individual and company, and never in a bland or generic format.

COVER LETTER FOR STUDENTS

420 Pape Avenue   **Chuck Carr**   **(416) 555-6666**
Toronto, ON M3S 1C5   cjcarr50@hotmail.com

May 7, 2007

Dear Mr. Lonergan,

As you can see on the attached résumé, I have worked in the Graphics Design industry in the past year as a co-op education student for the Shell Graphics & Design company of Toronto.

This is an area that I have been interested in for several years. Thanks to the experience I got at Shell Graphics & Design, I know that I want to work in the industry and am looking for an entry-level position on a part-time, full-time, or contract basis.

I've looked at your website, and some of the sample work you list there is similar to what I worked on at Shell Graphics & Design. In that work I used Adobe Photoshop, Illustrator, and InDesign on both Mac and Windows operating systems. I also used many of the most popular business software packages.

I can give you references from several employers that I have worked with on a part-time basis during my years at Leaside High School. They point out that I am a reliable and hardworking individual.

I am willing to work for you for a week without pay to show you what I can do. I will follow up with you by telephone within a week. Or, if it is more convenient for you, please contact me at the telephone number or email address shown above.

Sincerely,

Chuck Carr

Tell your students to send their marketing documents to an individual and never to a title like "Manager."

If they don't know the name of the individual in the department or company that they're sending the material to, they need to find out what it is through the company website or by calling the company. And, of course, they need to be very clear about the spelling of the name.

Sample twenty-first century résumé for students

The format of the twenty-first century résumé is one page, regardless of how much experience the individual has. The sender is not applying for a job; they're in marketing mode and trying to get the attention of the person they're sending it to. See Sample 17.

To do that, the sender must decide on what part of their background will be of interest to the recipient and not give them their whole life story, as many résumés do.

At the beginning the résumé should include a profile that is succinct, proactive and describes who the sender is, their experience and some indication of the skill set they have to offer. If students speak more than one language, that should be included in their profile.

Under "Experience" they should list what they feel is relevant and of interest to the recipient. They should include any voluntary experience or work they've done if it is appropriate. Include any projects they worked on in high school if they are relevant. Also include in this section any achievements if these are relevant.

Under "Work History" they should include the website address of the companies or organizations they've worked for, assuming they have one. This makes it easy for the recipient to quickly find out something about these companies if they're not familiar with them. Under "Education" they should include any training received from voluntary organizations they've worked for, if it is relevant.

Do not include "References will be supplied on request," since this is redundant. Ditto for hobbies and personal interests, unless these are clearly relevant to the type of work they're looking for.

Sample 17
TWENTY-FIRST CENTURY
RÉSUMÉ FOR STUDENTS

420 Pape Avenue   Chuck Carr   **(416) 555-6666**
Toronto, ON M3S 1C5   cjcarr50@hotmail.com

A Leaside High School graduate experienced in Mac and Windows computer operating systems, familiar with most popular business software packages. Looking for work in the Graphics Design industry on a part-time, full-time, or contract basis.

Experience

Worked for the Shell Graphics & Design company of Toronto on a co-op education basis during my final year at Leaside High School. Gained experience on a variety of projects using Adobe Photoshop, Illustrator, and InDesign on both Mac and Windows platforms.

Helped to create and produce the monthly Leaside Monitor student newspaper in my final two years at high school.

Worked as a Day Camp Leader for the Toronto YMCA in the summer of 2005 and 2006, supervising 8- to 12-year-olds in daily activities, including regular field trips to popular Toronto sites.

Work History

Shell Graphics & Design, Toronto, Ontario   2006–2007
www.shellgd.ca

Co-op Education Intern
Toronto YMCA   Summer 2005 and 2006
www.ymcator.ca

Day Camp Leader
Safeway Canada   2005 to Present
www.cansafeway.ca

Part-time stock and inventory assistant

Education

Graduate, Leaside High School   June 2007
YMCA Leadership Training   Summer 2005

SELF-COUNSEL PRESS — HOW TO FIND WORK IN THE 21ST CENTURY 09

Sample brochure for students

Creating a brochure is optional, but even if your students don't actually plan to have one printed up, the exercise of creating one similar to Sample 18 is beneficial in that it forces the student to define what they have to offer and how that could benefit potential employers.

To create a brochure, you would take what is shown in the sample and print that information on both sides of standard printer stock, using the standard colors printers use: red, black, and blue. Depending on the equipment and expertise you have available to you in your school, you may be able to create the brochure in-house; otherwise you would have to get it created at a printer.

Having an effective brochure will make your students stand out in a positive way from their competition. A brochure could be an effective way to get the attention of employers at a career fair or a networking event.

Creating rhetorical questions on side one that are effective and not obvious or silly is a challenge for experienced people, let alone a high school student. So you'll have to pay particular attention to this part of the brochure.

If your students are tempted to get really creative and produce a brochure on glossy paper with pictures and fancy graphics, while in theory this might have some appeal, in practice, such a brochure can be expensive to produce. So use your own judgement as to whether this is justified or not, depending on how much it will cost.

Simple and businesslike are the key considerations in determining what the brochure should look like and what it should contain. Much of the information will be the same or similar to what is in the other marketing tools.

Sample website for students

Creating a website is again optional, but considering how computer literate many students are today, doing so might appeal to them. What is shown in Sample 19 could also be created in a PDF file instead of a website.

The page shown in the sample would be the home page of the website. And you will notice that it is similar to page one of the sample

Sample 18
BROCHURE FOR STUDENTS

Side Two

Chuck Carr

A Leaside High School graduate experienced in Mac and Windows computer operating systems and familiar with most popular business software packages. Looking for work in the Graphics Design industry on a part-time, full-time, or contract basis.

Work Experience

- Worked for the Shell Graphics & Design company of Toronto as a co-op education intern during my final year at high school. Gained experience on a variety of projects using Adobe Photoshop, Illustrator, and InDesign on both Mac and Windows platforms.

- Helped to create and produce the monthly Leaside Monitor student newspaper in my final two years at high school.

- Worked as a Day Camp Leader for the Toronto YMCA in the summer of 2005 and 2006, supervising 8- to 12-year-olds in daily activities, including regular field trips to popular Toronto sites.

- Have worked on a part-time basis for the past three years for Canada Safeway as a stock and inventory assistant.

(416) 555-6666
cjcarr50@hotmail.com

Side One

Chuck Carr

A Leaside High School graduate experienced in Mac and Windows computer operating systems and familiar with most popular business software packages. Looking for work in the Graphics Design industry on a part-time, full-time, or contract basis.

- Could you use a reliable, hardworking high school graduate in an entry-level position in your company?

- Do you have experienced people doing basic computer work that could be done by a more junior employee?

- Could someone with Adobe Photoshop, Illustrator, and InDesign experience be put to good use on some of your current projects?

If you answered yes to any of these questions, I would appreciate an opportunity to meet with you to discuss how I might be able to help you.

(416) 555-6666
cjcarr50@hotmail.com

Sample 19
WEBSITE FOR STUDENTS

Chuck Carr

[Work Experience]   [Contacts]

A Leaside High School graduate experienced in Mac and Windows computer operating systems and familiar with most popular business software packages. Looking for work in the Graphics Design industry on a part-time, full-time, or contract basis.

- Could you use a reliable, hardworking high school graduate in an entry-level position in your company?

- Do you have experienced people doing basic computer work that could be done by a more junior employee?

- Could someone with Adobe Photoshop, Illustrator, and InDesign experience be put to good use on some of your current projects?

If you answered yes to any of these questions, I would appreciate an opportunity to meet with you to discuss how I might be able to help you.

[Work Experience]   [Contacts]

SELF-COUNSEL PRESS — HOW TO FIND WORK IN THE 21ST CENTURY 09

brochure. That's by design. You're really presenting the same information in electronic form. The "Contact" link would lead to information such as a cell phone number and email address. (High school students are advised not to post their home addresses online.)

Having a website or PDF file makes it easy for students to send their information via email to potential employers. However, they need to be very selective about this, since unsolicited email is considered "spam" and therefore frowned upon by some people.

Students must never be tempted to resort to emailing their website URL to a large number of employers, because this truly is "spamming" and could come back to haunt them. They may not know that the Internet service provider they have their email account with can terminate their account if they receive complaints that the student is "spamming."

The same rules that apply to all the other marketing tools apply here. The only employers they should be contacting are the ones they've done some research on. They should be fairly confident that the employer would be interested in the skill set they have to offer.

If your students are very proficient in web design, they may view the sample given as pretty boring and in need of spicing up with Flash or other fancy graphics. Steer them away from this. Simple and businesslike are still the guiding principles in designing the website or PDF file.

Students must also thoroughly test the website or PDF file to ensure that it doesn't contain any broken links or other technical problems, which would certainly create the wrong impression with anyone they send it to.

Things to Think About

Whatever endures can be created only gradually by long-continued work and careful reflection.

— *The I Ching*

"The unearned advantages of having been born as Canadians or Americans may be about to evaporate." This perspective from management expert Tom Peters (writing in *Maclean's*, December 1, 2003) referred to in Chapter 1 of the book is turning out to be prophetic and refers to all western countries, not only Canada and the United States. People in western countries have taken those "unearned advantages" for granted for decades and are having great difficulty in accepting the fact that they are evaporating.

In an article in *The New York Times* on July 19, 2008, under the heading of "Uncomfortable Answers to Questions on the Economy," Kenneth S. Rogoff, a professor at Harvard University and a former chief economist at the International Monetary Fund, said "The open question is whether we're in for a bad couple of years, or a bad decade." It also pointed out that many economists who previously thought that the frequent gloomy forecasts about the economy were overblown, had changed their minds and now felt that the situation looked grim and that the worst was probably still ahead.

If you looked at the forecasts on the economy from government officials, economists and many notable commentators in the media in the year prior to the mid point of 2008, you would see that they consistently overstated the health of the economies in western countries and that they had to lower their forecasts as the data showing what was actually going on in the economy became available. In an August 10, 2008 report in *The Observer*, the Confederation of British Industry (CBI) said "The CBI, along with most other forecasters, has been consistently over-optimistic about the economic outlook over the past 12 months." It went on to say that the UK economy was deteriorating at a faster rate than had previously been predicted. In Ireland, the annual increase in unemployment claimants as of August 2008 was the steepest since records began in 1967, according to a report in *The Scotsman*, September 7, 2008. This at a time when the Irish government was insisting that it was "better placed than most to meet the challenges ahead."

One of the fundamental facts associated with the Great Depression of the 1930s is that it was preceded by what was known as the "Roaring Twenties." Right up to the Wall Street Crash in October 1929, people were in denial about the realities of the economy and would not accept the fact that the good times were about to end.

In the same *New York Times* article referred to above, Alan S. Binder, an economist at Princeton University and a former vice chairman of the board of governors at the US Federal Reserve, stated that "We haven't seen this kind of travail in the financial markets since the 1930s." These types of statements from people of the caliber of Mr. Binder, comparing the economy of 2008 with the 1930s, are appearing more frequently in the media. They're not predicting another Great Depression but they consistently say that you have to go back that far to find anything comparable to current conditions. And while many commentators were predicting that the current downturn would be over in 2009, the horizon for the recovery keeps getting pushed out further and further. Yet the debate about whether or not the US economy is in a recession continues. If someone like Kenneth S. Rogoff can't determine if the economy is in for a bad couple of years, or a bad decade, the average person shouldn't feel bad if they're having trouble making sense of all the data being thrown at them.

Coming to terms with bad news doesn't come easily to us but it's in our own self-interest to face up to the reality of what is going on in the economy. Like it or not, we must face the fact that for years some governments, a significant portion of industry, and the public have been living beyond their means and now we have to pay the price for that. We've become a society that seems to be incapable of facing up to the harsh reality that good times don't last forever and that going through tough times is a part of the natural cycle of life and the economy. Losing your job or your home or your savings is very hard to deal with but deal with it we must just as our ancestors had to in their time. Nobody knows how long the economic downturn will last or how deep it will be but there are some changes we can make now to get us back on track.

Official unemployment statistics

There is probably no other statistic issued by governments in western countries that is more misleading and underestimates the scope of the problem than the monthly unemployment statistics. This is a serious problem because these same statistics are among the most closely watched and are the basis on which government policies and action on unemployment are based.

They don't come close to accurately measuring the true level of unemployment and they ignore what is a major challenge for a growing segment of workers: underemployment. According to a July 30,

2008 report in *The New York Times*, there were 5.3 million people working part-time involuntarily in the US. These are people who have had their hours reduced by their employers, or who cannot find full-time work. This category had increased by over 1 million in the previous year. The unemployment statistics area needs to be completely overhauled and we need statistics that are an accurate measure of what is going on in the workplace. But that is not going to happen. No elected politician is going to voluntarily change the status quo and produce new statistics that show that unemployment is a much bigger problem than the current statistics show. They would be committing political suicide if they did.

The only way we will get any progress on this problem is for the public, and particularly the unemployed and underemployed to become more vocal about the issue and demand that more funding and help be given to this area. Unless we become proactive and stop sugar-coating the facts, we'll never move ahead. The mainstream media can help too by being far more diligent and critical in their reporting on this issue. Too often they simply report the data supplied by governments without looking behind the numbers to get a better reading on what is going on. For those with the resources to do so, it would be helpful for them to conduct their own survey of the unemployment situation and report on their findings compared to what the official statistics are saying.

Secondary and post-secondary education

Not so long ago anyone who graduated from a college or university could expect to find a decent job within a few months of graduating. Now we've become very complacent about graduates either being unemployed or ending up in jobs they could have got without attending college or university. We need to end our complacency on this issue. If the best and brightest of our young people who have the brains and fortitude to graduate are unemployed or underemployed, why is this happening? We can't afford to squander one of our most important assets.

Is it because our colleges and universities are out of touch with today's workplace and keep turning out graduates who expect someone to offer them a job? Should we instead turn out graduates who understand that there's no law that says that anyone is going to offer them a job? That they will have to create their own job and make sure that they know how to do that?

Is it because our whole education system is still job centered while the workplace graduates are entering is anything but that? Do we need a whole new breed of educators who understand today's workplace, have experience in it, and who can adequately prepare our graduates to succeed in it?

Is it because we have our heads stuck firmly in the sand about the consequences of outsourcing and keep on waiting for the next great surge of job creation to take place? Are we happy to listen to the empty promises of politicians who tell us that they will bring back all those good jobs that have gone overseas? Is it too much to accept the fact that we're not just competing with China and India for jobs? That our competition now includes Argentina, Brazil, Chile, Egypt, Hungary, Indonesia, Malaysia, Mexico, Poland, Russia, Thailand, Turkey, and elsewhere?

Are we incapable of accepting the fact that for an increasing number of workers the era of the traditional job and all the security that came with it is over? Can we accept the fact that throughout history people have earned a living without jobs and that millions continue to do so?

The road ahead

Obviously we have some serious challenges ahead of us. As daunting as they may seem, we wouldn't want to trade them for the challenges our families faced in the twentieth century. They survived two world wars and a global depression that lasted for ten years. But they did survive all of that and so too will we survive the challenges we now face.

We need to stop trying to tackle this century's problems with last century's solutions. Albert Einstein observed, "The significant problems we face cannot be solved at the same level of thinking we were at when we created them."

We're in a new era in the workplace and we need to come up with new and creative solutions that are appropriate for this era. And we need to tap into the same built-in strength our forefathers had that got them through the tough times they had to deal with.

7

MANAGING YOUR CAREER

The destinies of men are subject to immutable laws that must fulfill themselves. But man has it in his power to shape his fate, according as his behavior exposes him to the influence of benevolent or of destructive forces.

— The I Ching

Career Management

Regardless of the changes that have occurred in the workplace in recent years, you could argue that it has always been in the best interest of the individual to look out for themselves and that taking ownership of the need to manage their career is the smart thing to do. That sounds logical enough, but many people don't know how to manage their career and further, they assume that their employer will do it for them.

That may sound naive to many people, but the fact is that traditionally employers have managed the careers of their employees and some still do. If you talk to people who have been in a stable job for years, they may never have given the idea any thought at all. It is something that employees have often taken for granted as being part

157

of the package that comes with having a job and again, many still think that way.

People who have lost what they thought were permanent jobs will see such an attitude as outdated and out of touch with the realities of today's workplace, forgetting the fact that they probably thought that way before they lost their job. Here we have a good example of the paradox of today's workplace. How you see it will be directly related to your experience in it.

If you have lost your job, you will probably buy into the popular notion that being loyal to your employer is a thing of the past. If you're one of the many who still have a steady job in an industry that is growing, you'll probably take the opposite view and be quite comfortable in being loyal to your company.

This raises an interesting question. How would you advise a young person who is about to enter the workplace about what their attitude should be toward managing their career? The answer will be influenced by your own experience and your opinion on where you think the workplace is headed.

The job and all it traditionally entails is far from being dead in spite of volumes of opinions that tell us it is. That being said, if you currently have a job and you're doing nothing to prepare yourself for the possibilty that you could lose it, you may be setting yourself up for a major disappointment.

In this section, we will take the position that regardless of what your current employment status is, it is in your own interest to assume the responsibility for managing your career. If you have always believed that your employer will do it for you, you need to rethink your position. Given all of the turmoil and uncertainty that is going on in the workplace, it makes little sense to assume that somehow you are going to be unaffected by it.

In spite of all of the evidence to the contrary, many people still can't face the possibility that their world could be turned on its head through the loss of their job. It's quite common, even in companies where downsizing is going on all around them, for people to convince themselves that somehow they're not going to be affected by it. They find ways to rationalize that their department, division, branch, or whatever is doing well and therefore will not be affected.

These are the people who are in deep trouble when they do lose their job. It's only after the loss that they realize how dependent they were on their company and how ill-prepared they are to find alternative employment.

The smart and realistic position to take is to at least acknowledge the possibility that you could lose your job. Ask yourself if there is anything you can do to make yourself more valuable to your employer and begin to prepare yourself for the worst-case scenario where you do find yourself unemployed.

Being informed and facing the realities of today's workplace is the best position to take. A company can survive without you, so you owe it to yourself and your dependents to prepare yourself for that possibility.

If you are a graduate entering the workplace and you land yourself what appears to be a plum, stable job, don't rest on your laurels. Look around you and you'll see many talented people who used to have what you have and through no fault of their own and for a variety of reasons lost their job.

You can't make yourself immune to the possibility of losing your job, but there are things that you can do to decrease the chance of it happening and to prepare yourself for survival in the event that it does happen to you.

Become career fit

In Chapter 2, just before the exercises that define your personal and career profile, you were given a quiz to determine how career fit you are. Go back to look at your answers and ask yourself how prepared you are to find work if you suddenly found yourself out of a job. This applies to college and university graduates too. To become career fit and to maintain your fitness, there are some things that you need to do on a regular basis.

Manage your career

Managing your career is your responsibility whether you are employed, unemployed, or underemployed. If you've been employed by the same company for a number of years and you've never given this any serious thought, consider getting some professional help and advice on how to go about it.

Go back to the exercises where you defined your personal and career profile and review them. Are you confident that you know your strengths, weaknesses and interests and where you want to go in your career, or could you use some help to further refine these? Shop carefully if you decide to get some professional help; make sure you are comfortable with the counsellor you choose and their experience and qualifications.

Many people wait until they lose their job before seeking this type of help. Getting it when you are employed makes more sense, and it may even decrease your chances of becoming unemployed. Most colleges and universities offer part-time courses in career planning and assessment, and some offer counselling services to the public.

If you don't have a written career plan, get some help in putting one together.

Sharpen your communication skills

Being competent in your field and having current skills are no guarantee that you will find work. If you have poor or mediocre communication skills, you could lose out to people who are less skilled than you but who communicate in a more compelling and persuasive manner.

In today's workplace the onus is on the individual to catch the attention of potential employers whether you are communicating with them by computer, telephone, fax, in person, or in writing, so make sure that the way you communicate in any of these modes is effective and businesslike.

Take advantage of the programs and courses available in your area that polish and strengthen communication skills. Finally, give serious consideration to joining a local Toastmasters International group.

Get connected

If you were asked to describe the important current issues and developments going on in your field or profession and where it is headed, could you do that? Do you subscribe to and continually monitor the main business publications in your area as well as the trade and professional magazines and journals that relate to your field? Which companies in your area are expanding? Can you name any new companies that started up in the last couple of months?

Which TV programs and websites that focus on workplace issues and trends do you watch and access on a regular basis? How many electronic newsletters that focus on the workplace and your field are downloaded to your PC on a daily, weekly, or monthly basis? What have you learned from them recently?

Stay current

If you are connected, you will know what skills are in demand in your field and the new areas and technologies that are coming onstream. Do you have those skills? Do you have a plan to obtain them? What programs and courses are being offered in your community over the next six months by colleges, universities, professional, and other groups that would increase your employability if you took advantage of them?

What professional development programs are being offered by the associations that you belong to in the next six months and which ones are you planning to attend? Are you on the mailing list of the colleges and universities in your area to receive their continuing education calendars and notices of upcoming career development programs?

Expand and cultivate your network

How many promoters and supporters are there in your network and how often do you communicate with them? What are you doing to expand your network, especially the promoters in it? Are you on the executive or actively involved in the associations that you belong to? Are there any associations that you don't belong to currently that could be beneficial to you if you did join them? What networking events are happening in your area in the next couple of months that you plan to attend?

What significant news on workplace activity did you pick up from your network in the past month? How many news items and job or work leads did you pass on to the people in your network in the past month?

Review your finances

An important part of managing your career is to take a fresh and innovative look at your financial situation, and to do that most people would benefit from the services of a financial planner. If you are new to self-employment or could be facing it as an employment option, you need to take a hard look at the financial implications of that on your lifestyle and how you manage your money. Unlike their parents, some college and university graduates will have to make their own plans for a pension upon retirement, even if they get a traditional job with a benefit plan. As noted earlier in this book, some employers are now excluding company pension plans from benefit packages for new employees.

In a July 19, 2008 article in the *Guardian* titled "A Generation in Denial," it pointed out that thirtysomethings and fortysomethings in the UK can't admit that they will face an impoverished retirement. In referring to this group as the "no-nest-egg generation," it pointed out that savings were their lowest in 50 years and nearly half of those in work had made no financial provisions for their retirement.

Even if you have a pension plan as part of your benefit package, it might not be the certainty you think it is. Some employers, in industries that are struggling, are getting permission from the courts to unload their company pension obligations as a way to stave off bankruptcy, which creates problems for employees who were taking their pension for granted. In an August 20, 2006, report in *The New York Times*, the City of New York estimates that its ability to meet its pension plan obligations for city workers is short by close to US $50 billion. Reports like this are becoming more common as organizations scrutinize their pension plan obligations more closely than they have in the past.

In his 2008 book *While America Aged*, author Roger Lowenstein says that America's impending pension problem is brutally simple: Private companies and governments have pledged to provide retirement income and health care for workers, but have not set aside the money to make good on their promises. In July 2008, as part of their attempt to stay solvent, General Motors announced that it would no longer pay for health benefits for their retirees over 65, something that had always been a part of their pension package.

Most peoples' lives are built around the assumption that there is a steady flow of income from a job. How prepared are you in the event that you lose that job, maybe for an extended period of time? Financial planners suggest that you should have at least six months' salary in your bank account and save around 10 percent of your income. Do you do that? If not, how would you survive a long period of unemployment?

Financial planning goes well beyond looking at cash flow and determining your income and expenses. You may have to take a broader look at your lifestyle and assumptions about how you'll survive in retirement, and you may have to generate alternative ways of earning your income. You may have difficulty replacing that one salary that has been your primary source of income for years and be forced to come up with more than one way to earn your living.

You may have to simplify your lifestyle. A spouse who may not have worked for years might have to find employment. Holidays, club memberships, and regular forms of entertainment that have long been a part of your life may now become luxuries that you can't afford.

If you live in an expensive neighborhood and have substantial equity in your home, it might make more sense to move into a more modest home, reduce your monthly expenses, and put the money currently tied up in real estate into revenue-generating investments.

Financial planning is an area where many people are weak, and they avoid facing it until they are in financial difficulty. Most of them would benefit from the advice of a qualified financial planner.

Take care of yourself

One of the growth industries in the 1990s was outplacement. Companies who lay off employees sometimes engage the services of outplacement companies to help their employees cope with the loss of their job and help them find alternative employment. These companies would also be doing these employees a favor if they paid for a one-year membership in a health club. The importance of maintaining healthy physical and mental conditioning in periods of stress is something that few people understand; if anything they tend to let these things deteriorate. You would benefit from increasing your overall conditioning regardless of your employment status, but it is of particular importance if you have recently lost a job or are in danger of losing one. It is difficult to make intelligent choices and maintain a realistic and healthy perspective on life when you are physically and emotionally drained.

Get in shape and see more of your friends, family, and positive-thinking, supportive people you know. Find a spiritual anchor, something that lets you see life from a broader, more philosophical point of view and instead of beating yourself up, remind yourself of your successes.

Become You Inc.

One of the interesting phenomena going on in the workplace today is the number of people who are going through the transition from being traditional employees to becoming self-employed as contractors or small business owners. Making the transition is a struggle for most people, which shouldn't come as a surprise when you consider that our society is one where the majority of people have earned their living from traditional employment for the past 100 to 150 years.

An ironic twist to all of this is that some of these people who struggled with the challenge to become self-employed, especially those who operate as contractors, are being offered full time jobs by the companies that they contract with. This often creates a dilemma for them. Regardless of their discomfort when they initially made the transition to self-employment, many end up enjoying it, and the idea of giving it up to become a traditional employee again doesn't appeal to them. They're torn between their new-found independence and the option to trade it for a more stable and predictable flow of income. That struggle is more common than you may think.

The issue of traditional employment versus self-employment also raises an interesting challenge for people who are entering the workplace for the first time. Which of these two options do you pursue?

Establish you inc.

As challenging as it is to become self-employed, the good news is that there are lots of resources available to help you. There are numerous books and websites on the topic, and most colleges and universities offer courses and seminars on how to set yourself up. You may even qualify for government assistance to attend some of these.

There are also many associations and groups of self-employed people and entrepreneurs that you can, and should, seriously consider joining. It makes little sense to try this on your own when you can have access to and learn from those who have already done it. These groups also are great for networking and as support for those who are new to self-employment.

In the US, the United States Association for Small Business and Entrepreneurship might be a good place to start. See www.usasbe.org.

In Canada, there is an association of student entrepreneurs called ACE-Canada. You can look at their website at www.acecanada.ca and pick up lots of useful information and tips. SIFE is an international association of student entrepreneurs; see www.sife.org. If telecommuting is something you are interested in or would like to explore, look at www.ivc.ca and you'll find a wealth of information on the subject. With a little bit of research on the web you may even find an association or group that specializes in your field of expertise.

Loyalty

If you currently have a job but are entertaining the possibility of becoming self-employed, you may be concerned that you're being disloyal to your present employer by seriously considering self-employment at the same time you're drawing a paycheck. As long as you're meeting your commitments to your employer you're not being disloyal to them; you're being practical and realistic.

Don't forget that if the management or owners of a company decide that it is in the best interest of the company to lay off you and some of your co-workers, that's what they'll do. They're not being disloyal to you and they won't enjoy doing it, but they won't hesitate to do it if it is in the best interest of the company.

Outsourcing

One of the common reasons for layoffs in companies is the decision to outsource some of the work to external contractors or companies. This is often done because it is cheaper and usually more efficient to do so. These companies often retain people whose skill set fits within the core competencies of the industry or type of work they do and outsource work that is of a more general nature. Sometimes they lay off people and hire them back as contractors.

If that were to happen in the company you're with, where do you think you would fit into all of this change? Do you possess a skill set that fits within the perceived core competencies or would it be easy for the company to replace you? If you don't have the skill set that they would tend to retain, is there a way for you to acquire those skills, assuming that you wanted to stay with the company?

What if the company announced that it wanted a workforce in several months that was made up primarily of contractors but before they went outside to hire people, they would give all current employees the first shot at being contractors? There's a catch though. If you want to be one of those contractors, you have to make a business case that shows the company that it's in their best interest to hire you. Give this scenario some thought and determine what your business case would be. If nothing else it will force you to look at your job from a broader perspective and evaluate how valuable you are to the company.

Increase your employability

One of the primary challenges in today's workplace, whether you currently have a job or are a contractor, is to develop a strategy for improving the skills you have to offer an employer or company.

Successful companies understand that they have to continually look for ways to improve the product or service that they offer to their customers. If you develop a similar mind-set with regards to the skill set you have to offer, you're more likely to be employed versus someone who is cruising along with a skill set that is not appreciating in value to their employer or potential employers.

Selling you inc.

Selling. This is at the top of the list of the things that people who are new to self-employment either hate or are very uncomfortable with. It's also the key thing that will determine your success or failure. There are a number of reasons for this discomfort, including lack of preparation, misconceptions about what it's about and failure to understand the effort needed to become proficient at it.

Professional salespeople go through months of intensive training before they're allowed to get in front of potential customers. In Chapter 2, you were given a series of exercises to determine exactly what you had to offer potential clients. How much effort did you put into those exercises? To do them effectively would have required a lot of time, thought, and revisions until you came up with answers that you were comfortable with and had internalized.

The foundation

Most people who are new to self-employment don't understand the need for this analysis, but it's the foundation on which your ability to sell effectively is built. It's the equivalent of the training that companies put their salespeople through. There are no shortcuts to this process and it's an ongoing challenge. Your comfort level in selling yourself will be directly related to how hard you worked at it initially and how much time you devote to perfecting it.

As an employee, you can get by with having a skill set that you apply to the tasks or work assigned to you. It's not that simple when you're self-employed. You still need that skill set but unless you can persuade someone to purchase it, you have nothing to apply it to. So, go back to Chapter 2 and honestly assess how well you prepared yourself. Until you get this part down pat, you're not ready to get in front of a potential client.

Effective selling

Another reason why people don't like selling is that they assume that they're not good at it and probably never will be. Some are uncomfortable talking about themselves and their abilities. It's not about acquiring the gift of the gab or fundamentally changing who and what you are. In fact, trying to be something you're not is the worst thing you can do. People will quickly pick up on that. Remember that by doing an effective job in Chapter 2, you will be miles ahead of the majority who either don't go through that process or, if they do, they do it superficially.

One of the keys to successful selling is also one of the simplest things to understand. You have to be genuinely good at what you do and be convinced that you can help the client you're talking to. They'll quickly pick up on that. Being sincere will go a long way to offset the lack of professional selling skills.

The last thing they want from you is a slick sales pitch. They'll be evaluating you on how well you know your subject, how effective you are in understanding their needs, and how you can help them. They won't hang you if you're not perfect but they'll quickly detect any effort to fake it, so don't ever do that.

If you're asked a question that you don't know the answer to, say you don't know. If it's important to the client and your chances of getting the assignment, tell them you'll get the answer and get back to them and be sure to do that as fast as you can.

Can you help them?

Whether or not you can help them is the key issue. They wouldn't be talking to you unless they had responded to your marketing efforts or had expressed a need for the service you provide. You're being given an opportunity to convince them that it's in their best interest to hire you. Here we come again to a point that has been emphasized several times, the need to polish your communication skills. While they won't be swayed by a slick sales pitch from you, you better be ready to describe what you do and how that will benefit them in a businesslike, persuasive manner.

Pick your brain

Be careful not to give your expertise away. In your eagerness to show a potential client what you can do for them you may unwittingly tell them enough about how you can help them that, with some intuition and imagination, they can then implement your ideas without you. There are people who will exploit you if they get a chance to do it, so protect yourself.

In making your initial proposal to them, your challenge is to give them enough information to demonstrate that you have the expertise you claim to have and can help them without giving them the answers to their problems up front. If you sense that they are trying to pick your brains, don't be shy about telling them that you'll be happy to provide specific recommendations to their problems once you have a firm commitment from them that you will be paid for doing so.

Test you

Even if you have good marketing material that shows that you know your stuff and have a track record of helping clients, they may want to see a concrete demonstration of your skills before they commit to hiring you. For example, if you are an accountant, they may give you a copy of their latest financial statements and ask you to analyze them to see if you can detect any potential problem areas and show them how you would address those. If you know your stuff, you won't be intimidated by this; you'll welcome the chance to demonstrate your expertise. Just tell them enough that clearly shows them you can help them without solving their problems for free.

Show your stuff

Even if they don't give you a specific test, you might want to take the initiative and show them that you understand their challenges and can help them. For example, if you're aware of some productivity-enhancing techniques or procedures that they're not using, whet their appetite by showing them that you know about them and how to implement them into their operation.

If you've studied their website and the sites of their competitors and have spotted something that might improve their operation, tell them about it in general terms. Just be careful and diplomatic in how you communicate this information. Handled properly, it might seal the deal for you. Handled poorly, you might turn them off or make them feel uncomfortable.

This can be especially challenging for senior people or those who have more experience and expertise than the decision maker or business owner they're talking with. Their challenge is to impress the client with their expertise and assure them that their role will be a supportive one in improving their operation, thereby making the client look good. This must be done in a non-threatening manner.

Objections

Don't expect that they will agree with everything you're telling them. That won't happen regardless of how well you've prepared yourself so try to take a different tack. For each argument you have for buying your services, play devil's advocate and see how a client may come up with an objection to it.

Professional salespeople are grilled on this aspect of selling. One of the things salespeople need to know about is their competition and how they stack up against the product or service of their competitors.

They assume that a potential client will compare what they are offering to what they can get from their competitors so they have to be ready for the challenge. So do you.

Honestly try to assess who your competition is and what they have to offer. Never criticize your competition. Get the client focused instead on your strengths. Here's where all that preparation you went through in Chapter 3 to create your marketing materials will pay off.

Pricing

Here is one of the trickier challenges you'll face in selling yourself. Try to keep the initial discussions focused on determining the client's needs and how you can help them. The more comfortable you make them that you know what you're talking about and can help them, the less they will focus on your price but don't kid yourself, it will come up in the initial discussions and you have to be ready to address it.

You should be able to give the client a rough idea of what you charge on an hourly, weekly, monthly, or longer-term basis but emphasize that you need to have a clear understanding of their needs and how long it will take you to meet them before you can give them a firm quote on what it will cost.

If they are almost exclusively focused on the price of your services before you have even determined what their needs are, that could be a red flag. You need to be careful about taking on a client like that. A serious prospect will understand that you first need to determine what their needs are and your ability to meet them, and they won't have a problem with you taking some time to come up with a firm quote for your services.

Resilience

The final quality you have to acquire and develop to become successful in selling yourself is the ability to deal with disappointments and the loss of what you thought was a sure deal. Professional salespeople have to deal with it too; it's probably the toughest thing to deal with in sales.

You did everything right, the customer was genuinely interested in doing business with you, you were probably depending on the contract to pay bills, then at the last minute the whole thing falls apart through no fault of yours. It happens to everyone. It's part of doing business and you'll have to learn to deal with it. Bounce back and move on.

Also, regardless of how well you prepare yourself in Chapters 2 and 3, you're going to end up with egg on your face from time to time, especially in the beginning. Again, everybody goes through that and you have to learn to roll with it.

Clients will forgive you if you screw up a bit at times as long as they're comfortable that you're genuinely trying to help them and give them an honest deal. Which brings us to the final point. Never underestimate a client's ability to evaluate your sincerity. They're a lot smarter and more intuitive than people who are new to selling give them credit for.

APPENDIX

Where the needs of the world and your talents cross, there lies your vocation.

— Aristotle

Answers to Quiz 1: The Workplace

1. *Name some medium to large organizations that potentially could use your skill set and explain why you chose them.* If you can't name any organizations, you've got some work to do. In looking at potential organizations, put yourself in their shoes. Why would they be interested in you? What exactly do you have to offer that would be of interest to them? Who is the person in charge of the area you want to work in?

2. *Name some small (less than ten employees) organizations that you would like to work with and explain why you chose them.* Most of the work opportunities today are found in small organizations. They tend to belong to trade and professional associations, so you need to determine what those are, study their websites, and get all the information you can on them. Ask the staff in the library for help on this. If you subscribe to

a blog that is related to the area you want to work in, you could try to get feedback from your community about any organizations that might be hiring. Stress your willingness to work on a contract basis when you contact these organizations.

3. *Name some projects that are either underway or will soon be started that might provide employment opportunities for you.* Expand your thinking in looking for work. Don't just go to obvious places like the newspaper employment section, Internet job sites, career fairs and so on. Constantly keep abreast of what is going on in the area you want to work in. When you see that an organization has landed a big contract or is expanding, don't wait for them to begin to advertise for new employees. You know they'll need help, so contact them before they start advertising and get a head start on your competition.

4. *Your chances of finding work will be directly related to the number of want ads you respond to, the number of recruiting agencies you register with and the number of résumés or CVs you send out. True or false?* False. This is the mind-set many people have. Your chances of finding work will be directly related to how effective your strategy for finding work is. Forget about sending out lots of résumés or CVs. This doesn't work and will only leave you frustrated and discouraged. Focus on the quality of the marketing documents you're sending out, not the quantity. Spend 90 percent of your time strategizing around which companies you should contact and what marketing tools you're going to send to them. Spend the other 10 percent sending out your marketing tools and following up on them.

5. *Name the three most active sectors in the economies of the cities or areas you want to work in.* Go where the action is. Ask the staff in the library for help to determine what the most active sectors are, and make sure you monitor them regularly. This way, you will be ready pounce on any opportunities you see before your competition even knows about them.

6. *What are the key trends in the sectors you want to work in?* You need to get connected to the sources that tell you what is going on in these sectors and monitor them regularly. Find

out what networking events, trade shows, conferences, and so on are coming up, and make sure you attend them with your marketing tools in hand.

7. *Name some influential people in the sectors you want to work in.* The more you know about these sectors, the more you will know about these people. What are they saying about the sector? What are they saying about the needs of the sector and the challenges it faces? Are they identifying areas where there's a need for more workers?

8. *Where do the "players" in the sector you want to work in hang out? What associations do they belong to? What networking events are they likely to attend? Identify the trade shows and conferences coming up in the next six months that they are likely to attend.* You need to find out where these influential people congregate and get yourself out there to meet some of them.

9. *What are the best media sources for keeping you abreast of new developments in the workplace and in particular the areas you're interested in?* You need to know more about what is going on than the average employment seeker does. At least 80 percent of the employment opportunities are never advertised, so you need to learn how to sniff them out. You'll have to experiment to come up with the best sources. You'll find that some of them are pretty superficial and a waste of time.

10. *Name some websites that will keep you informed about the areas you want to work in.* Maybe the community in the blogs you subscribe to can help you with this. If not, ask the library staff to help you. Don't simply look at these websites; study them. Look at the links section; it's there for a reason. Look at the news section too. Who has been appointed recently? They may be useful contacts for you. Who is heading up the associations that are of interest to you? Watch out for announcements on new associations and special interest groups that would make sense for you to join and become active in. Use your imagination and don't just look for the obvious in determining what is going on in the sectors you're interested in. If a company's name keeps coming up in a positive way, you know there's action there, so maybe you should contact them.

They may be looking for new employees but not be advertising that fact in the traditional way.

11. *What are the best electronic and/or print newsletters that will keep you informed about the areas you want to work in?* These can be a key source for keeping you informed, so it is important that you take the time to find out what is available and have the relevant ones downloaded or mailed to you. Ask the staff in the library for help on this and solicit your blog community and other contacts to locate these newsletters.

12. *Can you think of an unmet need in the areas you want to work in that could be an employment opportunity for you?* You should always be on the lookout for these. With some imagination you may identify them from all the sources you're connected to, or you may actually run across commentaries on them from the well-informed people in the area you want to work in. They may write an article on the subject that will appear in a blog, on a website or in a trade or association journal or magazine.

13. *Outsourcing will destroy the workforces of countries in the western world. True or false?* Nobody knows the answer to this. Only time will tell. Outsourcing has already eliminated many jobs in the auto, steel, textile and other industries. If recent history is a guide, "destroy" is probably an overstatement. Despite the fact that millions of jobs have already been lost to outsourcing, western economies are still going strong, with new industries and jobs coming onstream. Our biggest problem may be complacency and ignorance on this issue.

14. *You've just joined the association that you know the "players" in your sector belong to. The executive has asked you to fill the vacant "program chair" position and you've accepted. In putting together the program for the coming year, identify three topics that you know will be of interest to the members.* Now you're going to find out in a hurry just how well you are connected to and informed about the area you want to work in. If you have followed all the suggestions given so far in this section, you won't have any trouble in identifying these topics.

Answers to Quiz 2: You, the Brand

1. *What are your most marketable skills?* Many employment seekers are vague on the answer to this; it's one of the biggest weaknesses they have. In today's world you must be very clear about what your marketable skills are and why a potential employer would be interested in them. That's why so much attention was given to this area in Chapter 2. If you took the time necessary to properly complete that section, you should know the answer to the question. If you have doubts about how to answer it, you need to go over Chapter 2 again.

2. *What skills would make you more employable if you acquired them?* Keeping your skills up to date is an ongoing requirement in today's workplace, regardless of what stage you are at in your career. This is necessary even if you've been in a stable job for years. The only security you have in today's world is in having a set of skills that your employer needs. If you're coasting and haven't done anything of note to update your skills, you could be one of the first to lose their job should your employer decide to outsource some work or reduce its workforce.

3. *What courses, seminars, trade shows, or other events are coming up in the next few months that will give you an opportunity to upgrade your skills?* If you're as connected as you need to be to what is going on, you'll know the answer to this question. Make sure you're on the mailing list of the colleges and universities in your area so that you receive their continuing education offerings and any special seminars or workshops that may be coming up. Ditto for the trade and professional associations related to your field.

4. *Identify some accomplishments in your life or career that would appeal to a potential employer.* You may be asked to talk about these in a job interview, so you need to be aware of them. Knowing what you've accomplished and feel good about is an important part of knowing yourself and contributes to a healthy self-confidence. The "appeal to a potential employer" part makes you think about the relevance of your accomplishments to them.

5. *What do these accomplishments say about you?* Again, having the answer to this question on the tip of your tongue is an important part of knowing yourself. People often make the mistake of being reticent about their accomplishments. To be an accomplishment, you must have worked hard to achieve it, and may well have had to take some risks in the process, which speaks well of you. So stop being so reticent. Having a healthy self-esteem is a good thing and a requirement for success in life.

6. *Identify some accomplishments or activities from your college/university years that would appeal to a potential employer.* These often play a critical role in the eyes of employers trying to get a handle on what type of person you are. Résumés or CVs often look alike in terms of applicants' courses, grades, and so on, and it may be in your extracurricular activities that the employer will spot something to separate you from your competition.

7. *What do these accomplishments or activities say about you?* How do you think an employer will interpret these? If you were asked this question in a job interview, how would you answer it?

8. *Name some people you admire and would like to emulate. Identify some of the characteristics they have that you would like to have.* Don't be surprised if you're asked this question in a job interview. It's one way of finding out what your values are and what is important to you. Having positive, inspirational role models that you can refer to in times of introspection during your life and career can be helpful in keeping you on the right path.

9. *What type of company would you like to work for? Name some of the attributes or values it would have that would attract you to it.* The easier it is for you to answer this, the less the likelihood that you'll end up with a company that's not a good fit for you. Hiring is a two-way street. It's not all about what the employer wants; it's also about what you want. No employer worth working for will be offended by you asking probing, intelligent questions about the company's values.

10. *Name some companies that have the values and attributes you just identified.* The longer your list is, and the greater your confidence in your selection, the higher the probability you'll end up with a company that's a good fit for you.

11. *Blogging is a great way to market yourself. True or false?* It could be. It depends on how well you understand blogging, how mature you are, how discreet you are, and how well you communicate. If the blogs you participate in are relevant to the area you want to work in and the community consists of professional people who are connected to that area, blogging could be great way to market yourself if your approach is polite, professional, and not self-serving.

12. *Write a job description for the type of job you would love to have.* This can be a useful exercise for synthesizing all the various elements involved in selecting the right type of work for you. Don't be too quick to prejudge what you can achieve here. On balance, people tend to underestimate rather than overestimate themselves and what they can accomplish.

Answers to Quiz 3: Networking

1. *What activities are coming up in the next couple of months that might be good opportunities for you to do some networking?* By now you should be connected to the sources that keep you informed about what is going on in your area. You need to monitor these regularly and be on the lookout for genuine opportunities to network. Beware of events that are promoted as being networking events. Many of these are a waste of time, and it's a safe bet that the people you want to connect with won't be in attendance. Instead they tend to attract people who are looking for work.

2. *If you attended a networking event full of the type of people you would like to connect with, what would they be talking about?* In exchange for having access to these people, you are obligated to keep yourself informed about what is going on in your area. If you're a recent graduate, these people won't expect you to be an expert on the leading issues in your field, but it's reasonable for them to expect you to at least be aware of what is going on in a general way. There's also the possibility that

you may have had access to some leading-edge thinking and ideas at your college or university. If so, you're in an ideal position to share that knowledge, which is the surest way for you to connect with these people.

3. *Outgoing, gregarious people make better networkers than quiet, reserved people. True or false?* False. People who don't see themselves as outgoing or gregarious commonly use this as an excuse for not attending networking events — but this is a mistake. If you think that way, you clearly don't understand what networking is about, and you need to go back over the section in the book on networking. Being an effective networker is an essential skill that you must develop to succeed in today's workplace.

4. *Successful networkers are givers who consistently share their knowledge with no expectation of anything in return. True or false?* There's some truth in this, but their motivation isn't entirely altruistic. In a broader sense, they know that sharing their knowledge, in the long run, is a smart philosophy to develop and that they, in return, will receive their fair share of help from others.

5. *Name at least one non-profit or charitable organization that could benefit from your time and expertise if you were willing to give it.* Being actively involved with a non-profit organization was one of the characteristics of successful networkers listed earlier in the book. You can be sure that there's at least one organization that you can contribute to in a way that is mutually beneficial.

6. *What trade, professional, or other such organizations would it be beneficial for you to join and get involved with?* If you want to meet the influential people in your field, you'll find them on the executive and committees of the associations related to your field. So find the one that makes sense for you to join and volunteer for an executive position or to serve on one, or more, of its committees.

7. *The best time to network is when you're unemployed, about to graduate or when your job or contract is about to expire. True or*

false? False, but this describes the mind-set of many employment seekers and their attitude towards networking. Networking should be a state of mind and something that is an integral part of your life and career. And the time to start networking is when you're in secondary school, college or university.

8. *The more networking events you attend, the higher the probability you'll find work. True or false?* There's some truth in this. Certainly if you're not getting yourself out into the community on a regular basis, you're doing a poor job of networking. But the key to success is in the quality of the events you attend. If you're regularly attending genuine networking events, if you're actively involved with an association in your field, and if you are an active volunteer, that's what will increase your chances of finding work.

9. *Is there a need for a new association or special interest group in your chosen field? Are you willing to get it started? Are you willing to be the president or head of it?* Yes, there is a need for such a group — there always is. And if you are willing to head it up or get it started, you can be sure you will be on the radar screens of the people you want to connect with.

10. *People who are shy about networking or are uncomfortable with it are often very helpful and accommodating to others who need help or information from them. True or false?* True. This is one of those quirks of nature. And if this description fits you, you don't understand networking. Networking is a professional interaction, not a desperate plea for help. If you're actively involved with an association in your field and are volunteering, you've earned the right to seek help from your peers.

OTHER TITLES OF INTEREST FROM SELF-COUNSEL PRESS

Finance & Grow Your New Business: Get a Grip on the Money

Angie Mohr, CA, CMA

ISBN: 978-1-55180-820-8

$18.95 US/$19.95 CDN

Entrepreneurs need to know how to measure the effectiveness of their operations, human resources, and marketing in order to pinpoint inefficiencies and maximize profits. This book outlines all the ways to raise capital and then make it work for you!

Many small business owners aren't able to take that next big step in expanding operations. This book shows you how to raise money to finance expansion, how to analyze key factors in your financial information, and develop ratios of return on investment that will indicate the direction you should take your business. *Finance & Grow Your New Business* explains, in easy-to-understand terms, how to get the money you need for your business, and how to grow your business profitably.

The Entrepreneurial Itch

David Trahair, CA

ISBN: 978-1-55180-735-5

$13.95 US/$17.95 CDN

Statistics say about two out of three small businesses fail within the first three years. Those are some very tough odds. And yet, every year, unsuspecting entrepreneurs show up at their banks asking for small-business loans. The problem is that far too many people go into business without doing thorough research into what it really takes to be successful. And the best way to do this is to learn from someone who has worked with hundreds of small businesses.

In this book, small-business accountant and author David Trahair lays out in plain language everything that no one else tells you about starting a business. Trahair stresses that it's important for most people to start their business first as a side job. Then, market and develop the business until it becomes strong enough to survive those crucial first years, and profitable enough to provide an income for the owner. Trahair also offers excellent tips on what the major franchisors will never tell you.

Study Smarter, Not Harder

Kevin Paul, MA

ISBN: 978-1-55180-741-6

$20.95 US/$22.95 CDN

- Use the genius inside you

- Expand your memory capacity 100 times

- Energize your brain

At work or at school, requirements rise higher and higher as competition grows fiercer. We are constantly challenged by having to acquire new skills and ideas as those we've learned become obsolete.

By mastering the seven basic elements of complete study skills included in this tenth anniversary edition, you can tap into your hidden potential for maximum performance and increased learning power.

CD Contents

The following are included on the enclosed CD-ROM for use on a Windows-based PC. The forms are in PDF and/or MS Word formats.

Checklists

- 1: Preparation
- 2: Marketing

Quizzes

- 1: The workplace
- 2: You, the brand
- 3: Networking
- Quiz answers

Samples

- Cover letter
- Marketing letter
- Traditional resume examples
- Twenty-first century resume examples
- Brochures
- Websites
- Weekly action plan
- Electronic resumes
- Envelope